HEROISM AND DIVINE JUSTICE
IN
SOPHOCLES' PHILOCTETES

MNEMOSYNE

BIBLIOTHECA CLASSICA BATAVA

COLLEGERUNT

W. DEN BOER · W. J. VERDENIUS · R. E. H. WESTENDORP BOERMA

BIBLIOTHECAE FASCICULOS EDENDOS CURAVIT

W. J. VERDENIUS, HOMERUSLAAN 53, ZEIST

SUPPLEMENTUM TRICESIMUM QUARTUM

JOE PARK POE

HEROISM AND DIVINE JUSTICE
IN
SOPHOCLES' PHILOCTETES

LUGDUNI BATAVORUM E. J. BRILL MCMLXXIV

HEROISM AND DIVINE JUSTICE
IN
SOPHOCLES' PHILOCTETES

BY

JOE PARK POE

LUGDUNI BATAVORUM E. J. BRILL MCMLXXIV

ISBN 90 04 04165 6

I am very grateful to my colleagues, R. M. Frazer, Jr., and Roberta Reeder, who read a version of this work. Particular thanks are due to Professor Hans Diller, who generously consented to read the manuscript of a total stranger and who saved me from embarrassing errors. I must add that I have not always followed the recommendations of these readers, and all responsibility is mine for the shortcomings of this essay. Finally, I owe no small debt of gratitude to Mary Egger, who typed the manuscript and read proofs.

Almost all critics of Sophocles have seen in him, if not an optimist, at least a fulfilled idealist, each of whose plays balances against its grim tragic vision a final assertion of goodness or justice or compensating beauty. Partly this is because of our historical knowledge.[1] We know Sophocles as a man of recorded piety and a good citizen, who served the gods and served the state. Above all we know him as a man of fortune, a success, whose excellence was recognized in his own lifetime. Of such a man one might expect a serene confidence in the ultimate goodness of things. Partly, too, I think, what clearly is in the three Theban plays influences our reading of the other four. Justice in *Antigone* and divine grace in *Oedipus Coloneus* are so manifest; Antigone and Oedipus in *Oedipus Tyrannus* are such attractive characters, whose very strength implies a faith in man's worth. It is plain that in these plays we are in the world of high tragedy, which compels us to look up and admire, and, if occasionally we are morally disturbed, to give emotional consent at least to its awesome beauty.

However, the peculiar thing about Sophoclean criticism is that, when it comes to the interpretation of individual plays, there has been so much disagreement about precisely what it is that is good or just or beautiful. Many critics have been tempted to read into Sophocles' plays messages almost Christian in their moral tone. Thus Bowra: "Sophocles allows no doubts, no criticism of the gods. Sometimes indeed they are hard to understand, but none the less men must assume that all is as it ought to be. If divine ways seem wrong, human ignorance is to blame. In the end the gods will be proved right."[2] It is not my purpose here to argue that the "pietists'" view of Sophocles' religious attitude seriously distorts their interpretation of every one of the seven plays. Certainly *Oedipus Coloneus* and *Oedipus Tyrannus* are concerned with

[1] An excellent discussion of our knowledge of Sophocles' life and personality is found in Wolfgang Schadewaldt's article, "Sophokles und das Leid," *Hellas und Hesperien* (Zürich and Stuttgart 1960), 231-47 = *Potsdamer Vorträge* 4 (1947). See also Albin Lesky, *A History of Greek Literature*, tr. J. Willis and Cornelis de Heer (London 1966), 271-76.

[2] C. M. Bowra, *Sophoclean Tragedy* (Oxford 1965; repr. of the first edition, 1944), 367. In contradiction to Bowra, G. M. Kirkwood, *A Study of Sophoclean Drama* (Ithaca 1958), 271, points out that Sophocles allows frequent expressions of doubt and criticism of the gods, as well as assertions of their benignity (see below, p. 36).

religion, and it may be, although I do not think so, that these plays make assertions of the gods' wisdom and benignity. But, whether or not Sophocles' gods are essentially benign, the pietists' interpretations often are thrown out of kilter by their perspective; their need to find at the core of each play a theological question is responsible for the embarrassment, special pleading, and question-begging that is all too common in discussions of the less-frequently-read plays.

In reaction to this it has fairly recently become fashionable to place the emphasis of Sophoclean drama on the hero rather than on the gods. But the reaction has been just that, tending to the opposite pole. It has taken all virtue from the gods and vested it in man. Cedric Whitman, the "hero-worshipers'" leading spokesman, has put it succinctly: "The more we look closely for a satisfying justice in the world, the more inevitably we are driven to disillusion and to the admission that justice is with man, not the gods; that man is more responsible than he dreamed, though in a different way; and that perhaps this very quality in man is a kind of divinity." [3] I believe that Whitman is nearer to the truth than the pietists, inasmuch as Sophocles' bias is humanistic. But again, I question whether a narrowly prescriptive view such as this is sufficient to comprehend Sophocles' ideological variety. Whitman's book, for all that it has helped bring a salutary balance to Sophoclean criticism, can be as Procrustean in its interpretations as Bowra's.

Of course, most critics have taken a middle road, or rather, they are eclectics (Kitto is a good example), finding Sophoclean idealism manifested now primarily in the hero, now in the gods. I believe that eclecticism is right and proper in Sophoclean criticism. There is no monolithic Sophoclean philosophy. But the interesting thing is that everything written about Sophoclean drama finds idealism somewhere. And this search for idealism has tended to obscure distinctions. Even Gordon Kirkwood, whose book on Sophocles is the most balanced and clear-sighted among recent critical studies, can call Deianeira a "great figure" and can talk of the "purity of her devotion to Heracles" as a "devotion to an ideal" which is comparable to Antigone's highmindedness.[4] Now, however appealing Deianeira may be, she is a fictional creation belonging to a different

---

[3] Cedric Whitman, *Sophocles: A Study of Heroic Humanism* (Cambridge, Mass. 1951), 21.

[4] Kirkwood, 175-77.

order from that of Antigone. She, and Tecmessa too, are a great deal more like Creusa in the *Ion* or Alcestis, or even Phaedra.

In fact, Sophoclean drama is a great deal more "Euripidean" than most people want to admit. We all have been thoroughly conditioned to the idea that all of Sophoclean drama is—as *Oedipus Tyrannus* and *Antigone* assuredly are—what I called above "high tragedy." By "high tragedy" I mean tragedy written in what Northrop Frye calls the "high-mimetic mode," one of the essential characteristics of which is that its hero is superior to his fellow men.[5] I am not about to assert that Sophocles was writing low-mimetic plots, or realistic fiction whose characters, like us, are all too human. For I believe that the extant plays of Sophocles manifest a considerable variety of intention and strategy. But it must be admitted that critics generally have been uncomfortable in their interpretation of the *Trachiniae*; and a primary reason for this is that it has no very satisfactory hero. An essential characteristic of high tragedy is that it compels no doubts about the justice of the order of things. Frye calls high-mimetic tragedy "the fiction of the fall of the leader." The hero is an exceptional man, whose downfall is intelligible because it is directly connected with his exceptional qualities.[6] By raising himself above the common herd of men he puts himself in an exposed position. On the one hand we are inspired by the nobility of such a hero's aspirations or his endurance of adversity. But since his destruction derives in some way from himself we can understand and accept it and are not outraged. This special relationship between the hero and his destruction is missing in the case of Deianeira, whose emotions are warm and generous, but ordinary and even homely, and who is almost entirely an innocent victim. It is hard to escape the conclusion that, in Aristotle's terms, her destruction is μιαρόν.

Aristotle's critical judgement misled him when, as he seems to do, he rejected this kind of plot as a means of artistic expression; for art need not be moral. But he was right to deny it the cachet of tragedy, for it is not tragedy as he defined it. It belongs to a different literary mode (to use Frye's terminology); and though it can be

---

[5] Northrop Frye, *An Anatomy of Criticism* (New York 1967; repr. of first edition, Princeton 1957), 33-34. Frye says, more fully, that the hero of the high-mimetic mode is superior in degree (rather than in kind) to his fellow men but not to his environment.

[6] Frye, 37-38.

effective, its effect is quite different. The admiration of Antigone's
strength, which is an important ingredient of our response to that
play, is absent in Sophocles' account of Deianeira's destruction,
and we are left with a disturbed sense of injustice and futility. It
seems to me that this feeling of disturbance and disquiet is a dominant effect of each of the non-Theban plays—certainly of the
Trachiniae, Ajax, and *Electra*. In none of these plays can anyone
without a strong religious bias find much evidence of the benign
working of divinity in human affairs. And something is "wrong"
with the hero or heroes of each one; that is, our admiration of them
at least is seriously compromised. Not only is Deianeira not reaching
up after some great thing in full consciousness of the possible con-
sequences; there is a suggestion that there is a subconscious,
irrational element in her motivation. She is preocccupied by her
female condition, and she is prey to sexual fears and fantasies
reminiscent of Phaedra's.[7]

In the case of Ajax, few critics have been willing to face the
implications of Ajax' madness and Athena's quiet amusement at it.
Ajax is made a clown, like the mad Lear, but earlier in the play.[8]
We first see him as a grotesque object of fun, stripped of all dignity,
and this colors our view of him for the play's remainder. This is not
to say that the theme of the *Ajax*, the choice of death over dishonor,
is not a tragic theme, but the element of the grotesque mocks the
tragedy and cheats it of its full impact. Ajax realizes this when he

---

[7] In my opinion the effort to make Heracles the play's major character is
the result of a desperate recognition that Deianeira won't quite do. We see
Heracles only at the end of the play and only *in extremis*. The picture of him
is very one-sided. There is no evidence of any mental conflict within him, and
it is hard to see him as much more than a self-centered brute. Any nobility
which some may profess to see is drawn from the traditional figure of Heracles, not from Sophocles' figure. The reason for Heracles' appearance at the
end of the play is not something I am confident that I understand, but I
suggest tentatively that he appears as an ironic comment upon the fears and
desires of Deianeira, with which the play has hitherto been concerned and of
which he is the object. A great problem is the anticlimactic quality of the
last scene; what happens in the scene has no particular bearing on Deianeira's
death. But it is noteworthy that in two of the seven surviving plays, the
Ajax and the *Trachiniae*, there is a change of direction and an oblique
movement away from a climax and away from the central figure.

[8] For a discussion of the theme of the grotesque in *Lear* and its contribution
to the play's bleak pessimism see Jan Kott, *Shakespeare, Our Contemporary*,
tr. Boleslaw Taborski (Garden City 1964), 87-124. In his recent book on
Greek tragedy, *The Eating of the Gods* (New York 1970-73), Kott says, 43-77,
that Ajax is humiliated and made absurd.

comes to himself, and tries to redeem his heroic stature, but he fails. The reason he fails is that he has gone as far as possible already. His frustrated attempt to kill his former friends is almost the ultimate gesture of self-importance. With suicide he tries to go one step further. As he himself says, in a world in which he is hated by his fellows and repudiated by the gods, suicide is the only means left to retrieve his lost dignity. But not even in death does he win recognition of his worth from gods or men. For the act of suicide in itself is a surrender of the self-sufficiency to which Ajax lays claim. It does not enforce or compel respect of others, but merely demands it; and it is dependent on the willingness of others to recognize and honor the extreme strength of character that it has required. This willingness Ajax does not find. The gods do not take notice of his final prayer that Teucer find his body in time to bury it; and the last third of the play is a bombastic, burlesque quarrel over his body. In the end he is beholden to the pity of his worst enemy for the privilege of burial.

Electra comes nearer to being a satisfactory Aristotelian heroine. No one can fault her strength or deny that it is successfully implemented. But she also comes nearer to moral infirmity. Her emotions are excessive, distorted by her degrading experiences; she confuses love and hate.[9] Hers is a mangled personality, and the play essentially is a study of abnormal psychology. A recent critic who sees the abnormality of Electra's personality but tries to explain it away, points out that the play "circles" the problem of the extent to which a hero's best qualities may be salvaged from the hellishness of his experience. He concludes that the play gives no clear answer.[10] On the contrary, it does; for Electra's success is the triumph of the destructive forces within her.

That Sophocles' thought has a negative side has not been entirely ignored. Two studies in particular should be mentioned: *Sophocles and Greek Pessimism* by J. C. Opstelten[11] and an influential article by Wolfgang Schadewaldt, "Sophokles und das Leid." [12] However, "pessimism" and "suffering" might describe Sophocles' treatment of Antigone as well as his treatment of Deianeira. If a difference in "mode" exists between the Theban plays and the three I have

---

[9] Charles Paul Segal, "The *Electra* of Sophocles," *TAPA* 97 (1966), 504.
[10] Segal, 543.
[11] Tr. J. A. Ross (Amsterdam 1952).
[12] See above, note 1.

discussed briefly above, these words are not adequate to distinguish it. Suffering may be felt by high as well as low (and in Schadewaldt's view Sophocles' heroes all are superior individuals who are refined by suffering and become "more themselves" because of it).[13] Pessimism can imply a vision of the good which is disappointed, and it is this that Opstelten sees as a pervasive attitude in Sophocles' thought (and in Greek thought in general).[14] I can think of no single word that might be substituted for "pessimistic" to describe what is distinctive in each of these three plays about Sophocles' conception of his heroes and their circumstances. It is variously pathetic, ironic, brutally realistic and perhaps a dozen other adjectives. The common quality in all three plays might be inadequately described as a lack of illusion. *Contra* Opstelten I can see in these plays no lofty visionary quality, but rather its opposite, the dismissal of the ideal as an object of consideration. The difference from the Theban plays that they share in common is that the poet is not demanding that his audience look up in admiration and awe, but that they look down.

* * *

I have chosen to write about *Philoctetes* because, perhaps more than any other of Sophocles' plays except *Oedipus at Colonus*, it seems on the surface to be affirmative and idealistic, even optimistic. In it both hero-worshipers and pietists find aid and comfort, for (1) it has an undeniably attractive and morally satisfactory hero, and (2) the play ends with a divine intervention which seems to provide a successful denouement. However, I shall try to show that Philoctetes, attractive as he is, is not a hero of high tragedy. He is too passive. He does not inspire the audience with a sense of wonder at man's potential greatness; rather he is the object of its sympathetic pity. He is an undeserving victim of misfortune, to whose warm personality we respond, and whom we want to see compensated for his sufferings. But the significant word is "victim."

---

[13] Schadewaldt, 244 (see below, p. 37).

[14] Opstelten, 207-208, calls Greek pessimism "a pessimism that has seen and learnt how dangerous a lofty desire for happiness is for man and with how little he ought to be satisfied." He adds that this is "a pessimism of insight rather than of temperament." A few pages later, 211, he says that, in tragedy, out of pessimism a kind of optimism emerges and, "In so far as the play turns on heroism the value in human feeling which we call 'optimism' is perhaps best explained as a 'belief in man and in his ἀρετή.' "

I shall try to show that the play's efforts are devoted to creating a sense of indignation at Philoctetes' suffering more than one of admiration of his resistance. To some critics the problem of Philoctetes' impotence and the suffering he has endured does not seem an important one, because they consider a reassertion of divine justice to be the play's primary concern. After all, the gods' purpose is to make amends to Philoctetes, is it not? However, as I shall argue, the validity of this interpretation depends almost solely on the *ex machina* ending. For until almost the end of the play it is not the gods' benevolence that is emphasized, but its opposite. Much of the play concerns itself with the question of the reason for the gods' willingness for Philoctetes to suffer so, and with a dramatic demonstration of the intensity of his suffering. As the play progresses, more and more it directs itself to the question whether Philoctetes' salvation, his return to the Greek army, will benefit him as much as it will benefit his enemies. The glory and reputation among the Greeks at Troy, which is the chief benefit that the gods will bestow upon Philoctetes, is shown long before the end of the play to be of no value to him. Philoctetes considers it not a thing of honor, but a thing of shame, to consort with and win repute among men whom he considers to be dishonorable. Thus the intervention of the god, which is essential to the pietists' interpretation of the play, in itself makes their interpretation a difficult one. For the *deus ex machina* directly reverses the whole movement of the play and is so inconsonant with it as to seem absurd.[15] Happy ending, nice and tidy.

Most critics seem to have felt the inappropriateness of the *deus* and have felt the need to apologize for it or explain it away. A few—two of these, paradoxically, among the most discerning—have simply abandoned critical responsibility, denying that the *deus* is functional. Thus I. M. Linforth, whose monograph is the most searching and sensible thing written on the *Philoctetes*, complains of Heracles' appearance as a "cavalier procedure," but explains that it is completely external to the action, an ending tacked on to make the play agree with the myth. He adds, "The plain fact is that the drama of Philoctetes' resistance to the mission of

---

[15] Karin Alt, "Schicksal und Physis im *Philoktet* des Sophokles," *Hermes* 89 (1961), 172, whose interpretation is of the pietist persuasion, compares Heracles' appearance here with the Euripidean *deus ex machina* and admits that it is as paradoxical as any in Euripides.

Odysseus is ended when he is about to sail for home ...." [16] Kitto, too, says that before the *deus ex machina* "... the logical design ... is complete." [17] This "logical design" to Kitto is the defeat of Odysseus and the Atreidae, Philoctetes' enemies. Kitto admits that their ends are furthered by the *deus*, but he asserts that we don't *feel* that this is so.[18] This, I believe, is an aesthetic error, not essentially different from an art critic's denying that a statue's head is missing which he considers to be disproportionate to the body. Kitto and Linforth dislike the dissonant ending, if I may shift the metaphor, and consequently they deny its aesthetic effectiveness.

It is to Kitto's and Linforth's credit that they did hear this dissonance and admit it. Many more critics have claimed that the *deus ex machina* is a continuation and culmination of the action of the play. Such critics must emphasize the importance of Odysseus' unsuccessful machinations in furtherance of the gods' oracle. Odysseus, the argument goes, attempts to use his knowledge of the oracle in order to manipulate it for the sake of success, but with his insufficient human understanding he comes to grief.[19] When Neoptolemus abandons deceit and attempts to persuade Philoctetes in all sincerity, it is too late. Finally, when human efforts fail the gods take a direct hand. What man has attempted in vain the gods accomplish.[20] Philoctetes' quick turnabout and consent to do what he hitherto has steadfastly refused to do is a problem because it is so sudden that it seems unmotivated. Some explain that it is not a sudden reversal of intention at all, for Heracles appeals to Philoctetes as a friend and not on the basis of authority; Philoctetes has been prepared for such an appeal by Neoptolemus' attempts to reach him through friendship and

---

[16] Ivan M. Linforth, "Philoctetes, the Play and the Man," *University of California Publications in Classical Philology* 15 (1956), 151-52.

[17] H. D. F. Kitto, *Form and Meaning in Drama* (London 1960), 136. First published, London 1956.

[18] Kitto, 136-37.

[19] According to Hans Diller, "Göttliches und menschliches Wissen bei Sophokles," *Gottheit und Mensch in der Tragödie des Sophokles* (Darmstadt 1963), 1-27 = *Kieler Univ. Reden* 1 (1950), man's attempt to exploit his knowledge of a divine dispensation is a characteristic theme of Sophocles' later tragedies. See pp. 20-21, 25-26 *et passim*.

[20] Bowra, 282-84, 299-301. See also B. M. W. Knox, *The Heroic Temper* (Berkeley 1964), 120; Eilhard Schlesinger, "Die Intrige im Aufbau von Sophokles' *Philoktet*," *RhM* 111 (1968), esp. pp. 103, 124, 155-156.

persuasion.[21] To others Philoctetes' sudden change of heart is an indication of his piety and his willingness to defer to the superior authority of heaven.[22] The god Heracles is able to explain to Philoctetes the meaning of the wrong done to him, as Neoptolemus, with his insufficient human knowledge, cannot, and Philoctetes' piety prevails over his hatred.[23]

I shall discuss later in more detail whether in fact the play ends in success, and whether the intervention of the gods does accomplish justice and happiness for Philoctetes. Here I want only to observe that if the appearance and speech of Heracles is intended to provide a spectacular and climactic resolution, showing the superior wisdom and benevolence of the gods, it is utterly unsuccessful. Kitto thinks it a colorless speech;[24] rather it is cursory and facile. It tells Philoctetes only that it is the will of the gods that he go to Troy where he will be cured and will be triumphant. Heracles tells Philoctetes nothing that Philoctetes has not heard before and rejected.[25] The issue that is at the source of Philoctetes' resistance, and on which the play's action turns, is whether justice ultimately exists in the world, why the evil prosper and the good suffer (see below, pp. 43-46). But the claim of some critics that the god explains

---

[21] See esp. N. T. Pratt, Jr., "Sophoclean Orthodoxy in the *Philoctetes*," *A J P* 70 (1949), 286-87, and Herbert Musurillo, *The Light and the Darkness* (Leiden 1967), 118.

[22] S. M. Adams, *Sophocles the Playwright. Phoenix Supplement* 3 (Toronto 1957), 135: "Philoctetes accords to heaven what he could not to any mortal."

[23] Antonio Maddalena, *Sofocle* (Turin 1959), 263-65. See also G. Perrotta, *Sofocle* (Milan 1935), 467; Robert Muth, "Gottheit und Mensch im *Philoktet*," *Studi in onori di Luigi Castiglioni* 2 (Florence n.d.), 648-49; Bowra, 306.

[24] Kitto, 105: "[The speech provides] not the inevitable conclusion of a tragic action which finds its catharsis in the illumination that it brings, but simply a satisfactory ending."

[25] Linforth, 150: "Thus Herakles requires Philoctetes to do precisely what he has persistently refused to do. But he speaks with total disregard of all that has occurred through the course of the play .... He speaks as if he were unaware of Odysseus' intrigue and Philoctetes' passionate resistance .... He says nothing to meet Philoctetes' objections, and he makes no promises for the future which Philoctetes has not already heard."
Andreas Spira, *Untersuchungen zum Deus ex machina bei Sophokles und Euripides*, (Kallmunz 1960), 27, believes that the *deus* does offer Philoctetes an additional incentive: glory (or, more specifically, that Heracles tells him that he has been prepared by suffering for glory). However, fame is a completely inadequate recompense for Philoctetes' suffering, for to him it is not of any value. And the suggestion that he will win glory if he goes to Troy has been made before, both implicitly and explicitly (ll. 997-98, 1344-47) and has been emphatically repudiated (see below, pp. 42-43). To him a return to the Greek army would mean not glory but shame (see below, p. 47).

the meaning of Philoctetes' suffering could not be further from the truth. The speech of Heracles completely ignores the question of justice (see below, pp. 50-51).

The *deus ex machina*, then, is a resolution which does not resolve; it is a *non sequitur*. This irrelevance, or pointlessness, is what prompted Kitto and Linforth to suggest the *deus* is "external" to the play—in other words, that it has no meaning. But can it not be that the pointlessness itself has meaning? The gods' casual disregard of Philoctetes' anguished questions about the reason for the existence of so much apparent injustice implies that they have no interest in them—which is to say that they have no interest in what has previously happened in the play.[26] Their achievement by *fiat* of their desires makes the struggles which have taken place on the stage, and over which the audience has agonized, completely inconsequential. The use of the *non sequitur*, the calculated absence of causal relationship between events, is a primary device of the modern theater of the absurd, which so often deals with the theme of the meaninglessness of life; surely in the mid-twentieth century this is a device that we should be able to appreciate. If the *deus ex machina* is not merely an artistic failure, if Sophocles did not for some reason in this short speech fail to say what he intended to say, then the playwright is thumbing his nose at his audience, and at mankind.

But assume for the sake of argument that the *deus ex machina* was a failure, and that Sophocles was attempting through it to indicate the justice and benevolence of the gods. It must be seen that if the *deus* is to be regarded as the completion of the previous action rather than as a reversal, then the focus of the play must be on Odysseus' machinations and Neoptolemus' efforts to implement them. In other words, the play must be a play of intrigue. This cannot be overemphasized: if the *deus ex machina* is to be considered the natural conclusion of the plot, like the appearance of Athena in *Iphigeneia in Tauris* or of the Dioscuri in *Helen* or of the sun-god's chariot in *Medea*, then it must accomplish the end toward which the actions of the important characters are directed. This means that in this play Odysseus, Neoptolemus, and their intrigue must be of first interest. Many critics have at least dimly recognized this, and it is common to speak of the play as a play of intrigue.

---

[26] See Opstelten [above, note 11], 220.

I am not about to say that intrigue is not of crucial importance to the plot. But clearly it is not of primary interest. Very few lines of the play are devoted to furtherance of the intrigue, and very many lines are devoted to Philoctetes' expressions of emotional reaction to what is happening to him and has happened. But, aside from this, a plot of intrigue requires (1) that the goal to be attained should be clear from an early point, and (2) that, if the details of the intrigue are not made known to the audience, at least the audience should be able to recognize each act as contributing to the achievement of its goal. This is notoriously not the case in *Philoctetes*. The full revelation of the oracle, defining the goal of the intrigue, is not given until almost the end of the play; and as late as line 1080, when Odysseus leaves the stage with the bow, there must be some doubt in the minds of the audience whether the conspirators' purpose is to obtain Philoctetes or only the bow. Certainly about Odysseus' strategy there is not only doubt but confusion. Even Eilhard Schlesinger, who emphasizes the importance of the intrigue, points out that in the first scene, contrary to the practice of Euripides, who is the great master of drama of intrigue, Sophocles fails to let us know precisely what Odysseus' plan is.[27] I submit that if we are honest with ourselves we must admit that at the end of the play we still do not know precisely what Odysseus intended. Most critics assert that at line 1080 Odysseus is bluffing, trying to get Philoctetes to follow. But do we know that this is so?

There are two or three points in the play at which the intention of one or other of the conspirators is unquestionably vague or ambiguous. Why at line 639 does Neoptolemus refuse to sail, saying that the wind is unfavorable? At line 526 he has implied that it *is* favorable. It generally is assumed that this is because Neoptolemus has a sudden attack of scruples, but Schlesinger believes that getting Philoctetes on board ship while he still is in possession of his weapons is the last thing Neoptolemus wants, and that it cannot be part of Odysseus' plan.[28] What then was Odysseus' plan? Why does Odysseus send the false merchant, if not to hurry Philoctetes on board ship? Why at line 839 does Neoptolemus state to the chorus, which is urging him to take the bow and run, that the bow

---

[27] Schlesinger, 110. In a note Schlesinger refers to H. Strohm, *Euripides, Interpretationen zur dramatischen Form. Zetemata* 15 (Munich 1957), 64 ff.
[28] Schlesinger, 114-15.

is worthless without Philoctetes himself? Does he suddenly see, as some say, that Odysseus is wrong and that to steal the bow is to cause their mission to founder? [29] Or is he acting out of more general humanitarian reasons? [30] These points of vagueness have been worried over many times by critics who have realized instinctively that they should not exist in a drama of intrigue, and who have answered their own questions with a distressing arbitrary positiveness; distressing because it obscures the fact that the answers are not given in the text of the play itself. I assert that the vagueness is there because Sophocles does not care about the mechanics of the intrigue at all; and the obvious reason for this is that the intrigue is not the focus of interest, but lies in the background. The plot does not move toward the attainment of the object of the intrigue; rather the fact of the intrigue only initiates the real action of the play. The focus of interest is Philoctetes who, with his generous and mercurial emotions, dominates the stage from the moment he enters. The play is about Philoctetes', and to a lesser extent Neoptolemus', reaction to the deception, as well as to the wrongs done to Philoctetes in the past which are of a kind with it.

* * *

A few pages back I suggested that one of the reasons why Sophoclean critics feel at home with this play is that the attractive, vividly drawn protagonist is of the type considered to be the hallmark of Sophoclean drama. He is a much more satisfactory hero than either Ajax or Heracles, whose personalities are veiled by their reticence, and unlike Electra's his basic moral soundness is not open to question. In fact, in the extravagance of his emotions, his generosity and good-will, he is more like the Oedipus in *Oedipus Tyrannus* than any other Sophoclean hero. Because his emotions are so intense, his likes and dislikes so pronounced, and his conviction of the wrongs done to him so unshakeable, it is tempting to see in him the strong-willed, self-assertive hero who belongs to high tragedy. The vigor and forcefulness of his personality after so much suffering have often been admired. "There is an indurate

---

[29] Alt [above, note 15], 158-59; Bowra, 281; Karl Reinhardt, *Sophokles* (Frankfurt-am-Main 1947 ³), 190-91; Adams, 150, 154.

[30] Linforth, 130; Georges Méautis, *Sophocle: Essai sur le héros tragique* (Paris 1957), 80-81.

quality," says Norman Pratt. "But he has endured and has maintained his intellectual vigor. He shows breadth of sympathy, affection, even tenderness toward Neoptolemus. There is an eager spirit and sensitivity to kindness." [31] From here it is only a step to the idea that these are exceptional qualities of character that lie at the source of his near-tragic decision—the implication being that it is his own strength that places him within an inch of destruction. Thus Pratt can speak of Philoctetes' "greatness." [32] In the play itself Neoptolemus, in effect, calls Philoctetes hubristic (1316-21):

ἀνθρώποισι τὰς μὲν ἐκ θεῶν
τύχας δοθείσας ἔστ' ἀναγκαῖον φέρειν·
ὅσοι δ' ἐκουσίοισιν ἔγκεινται βλάβαις,
ὥσπερ σύ, τούτοις οὔτε συγγνώμην ἔχειν
δίκαιόν ἐστιν οὔτ' ἐποικτίρειν τινά.
σὺ δ' ἠγρίωσαι.

But we should not make the mistake of assuming therefore that Sophocles believes that Philoctetes is wrong—or even that the character Neoptolemus does so, for within less than 200 lines Neoptolemus has consented, at risk to himself, to support Philoctetes in his obstinacy. It is one thing to believe, as Neoptolemus clearly does, that Philoctetes is imprudent to refuse to yield to ineluctable forces, but it is another to think that the catastrophe threatening him is one of his own making.

Philoctetes' enforced isolation may call to mind the isolation of Achilles, and the influence of the *Iliad* on this play (the delegation headed by Odysseus, the threat to return home, etc.) has been remarked upon.[33] Going beyond these superficial similarities, P. W. Harsh has suggested that Achilles and Philoctetes are comparable in mental attitude.[34] But similarities between Philoctetes and Achilles, who may be considered almost the archetypal hero of high tragedy, are misleading. The briefest comparison will show that Philoctetes differs from Achilles fundamentally and generically. (1) Achilles exiles himself, while Philoctetes is a pariah. He does not set in motion the series of events that destroy him or make

---

[31] Pratt [above, note 21], 280.
[32] Pratt, 278.
[33] Schlesinger [above, note 20], 103-05, 114.
[34] P. W. Harsh, "The Role of the Bow in the *Philoctetes* of Sophocles," *AJP* 81 (1960), 410.

any free decision whatever until about line 1350 of a 1470 line play.
(2) Both Achilles and Philoctetes reject petitions to come to the
aid of the Greek army, but for very different reasons. Achilles' anger
initially and essentially is directed against only one man. As the
Iliad progresses he becomes increasingly alienated from his fellow-
men, but this alienation, rather than being deeply felt, is simply
a corollary of his ambition: he is dissatisfied with the honor given
him by the Greek army. His concern for his fellows, for their well-
being and for their opinion of him is obvious; if he had no such
concern there is nothing to stop him from sailing home, as he
threatens in Book IX. The conflict leading to Achilles' tragic downfall comes from within himself; it is compounded of contradictory
impulses to help his fellows and to isolate himself from them.
Philoctetes, on the other hand, despite Harsh,[35] is divided by no
such conflicting feelings. He does not, like Achilles, create his own
problem. The need to help the Greeks is imposed upon him by an
outside force—the will of the gods. He feels no inner compulsion
whatever to help the Greek army, because he has no fellow-feeling
for them at all. To his way of thinking the good among them have
died, and only the evil survive unscathed (403-52). He does not,
moreover, like Achilles, resist out of wounded pride or ambition
for something better; rather his resistance comes from a determination not to sink lower; to return to the Greeks would be to help the
evil and to seem to be like them (1371-72; see below, pp. 43-47).
Philoctetes', then, is a passive response to a purely external
initiative. (3) Achilles' decision derives from his dissatisfaction
with his lot as a man. He is conscious of his superiority to other
men; disillusion at their failure adequately to recognize true
excellence prompts his physical and emotional withdrawal from
them. Philoctetes, because of his brutal appearance (226) and his
odor (473, 481-83), has a strong sense of his own inferiority. He feels
that in the past he has been despised by other visitors to his island
who have bothered to grant him no more than casual charity
(307-11, 494-99). He wants nothing more than to be allowed to
return to the company of men. When Neoptolemus and his sailors
arrive he is pathetically glad to see them (234-44). And even after
he knows that the chorus of sailors have betrayed him, and he rejects
them with one part of his mind, he cannot bear to see them leave,

---

[35] Harsh, 408-10.

but begs for a few moments more of their company (1181-85, 1190).

So far is Philoctetes from being a man whose strength has raised him to an exposed position. It is true that near the end of the play Philoctetes does refuse to return to Troy in spite of knowing that this is the wish of the gods and even the decree of fate. Reckless and audacious folly probably is too mild a description of this defiance and it is reasonable to regard it as hubristic. But it seems to me that wir Philologen are much too inclined to be formulaic in our literary analyses; to look for the hubris, and, when we have found a place to attach the label, to regard the work in question as completely understood. Events fitting the formula should not be too much abstracted from the rest of the play. This, in large measure, is the reason for our difficulty in appreciating Euripides, who notoriously is the Greek tragedian most imitated by modern artists and least discussed by modern scholars. Philoctetes' defiance must be seen in the context of what has happened and what has been said before in the play—that is, in relation to his past sufferings. However, because we expect a moral judgement of the protagonist to be a basic concern of tragedy, the importance of Philoctetes' disregard of the gods' oracle and refusal to go to Troy, late as it occurs in the play, is vastly overemphasized. We are told that he suffers from the sin of pride (!), that he is blind, that he is deluded by his hate, that his understanding is insufficient.[36] He is even linked with Odysseus in his delusion and his all-too-human refusal to have anything to do with truth, which can come only from the gods.[37]

Now certainly delusion is a subject dealt with in this play. One of the pointed ironies is that the clever Odysseus is deluded in his choice of a course of action; but surely the most significant thing about Odysseus is that he is a man without conscience or any true concern for the good. To compare Philoctetes' mental and moral state in any way with Odysseus' is a serious misreading of the play

[36] Respectively: Maddalena [above, note 23], 260; Bowra, 291; Alt, 165, 169; Reinhardt, 200.

[37] Bowra, 263, 284-85; see also Alt, 173-74. Reinhardt's critical instinct enabled him to see that most of the play is calculated to make us feel sympathy for Philoctetes and anger toward those who wronged him; so that he did not make the mistake of equating Philoctetes' and Odysseus' guilt. But his need to see Philoctetes as more than an innocent victim led him to confusion and contradiction: Philoctetes is right as a "sufferer" but wrong as a "doer" (p. 195), whatever that means.

and betrays the all-too-Christian limitations of the critics' understanding. It is a judgement of an ethic that tends, at least, to
regard all sins as equal and believes (as Bowra does not scruple to
say in connection with this play[38]) that the divine can do no wrong.
No critic, except Harsh and those who follow him,[39] ever specifies
what it is that Philoctetes is blind to, or what it is in the big picture
that he doesn't see and understand, and the playwright himself
curiously omits to instruct Philoctetes or us on this point. The only
admonition made to Philoctetes that mentions defiance of the gods
warns, not that his understanding or his moral position is inferior,
but only that he is weaker. Neoptolemus (1316-17; see above p. 13)
says, It is necessary for men to bear the fortunes given to them
by the gods.

The critical myopia that concentrates on the last lines, where
Philoctetes is defiant, at so great an expense to the rest of the play,
and puts the guilt of the sufferer in the same category with that
of his persecutor, is due ultimately to a failure to classify this play
generically, or, as Frye would say, according to mode. The play
belongs not to Frye's high-mimetic mode (see above, p. 3 and
note 5) but to what he calls the "ironic" mode. The hero of the
ironic mode is not superior to ordinary mortals, but is inferior in
power, "... so that [when the plot is a tragic one] we have the
sense of looking down on a scene of bondage, frustration, or ab-
surdity." [40] Philoctetes, vivid as his personality may be and out-
spoken as he is, is much more like Deianeira in his inability to
help himself than like Oedipus.

From line 33, when Neoptolemus describes to Odysseus what he
sees inside Philoctetes' cave, it is apparent that Philoctetes' is a
different world from that of Oedipus, secure in his proud Thebes,
surrounded by loyal subjects. Neoptolemus speaks of a bed of
leaves, a rough wooden cup, kindling wood, and pieces of cloth
stained with pus, spread out to dry. Philoctetes is a pitiable figure,
a "Euripidean" hero dressed in rags. At his first appearance, before

---

[38] Bowra, 284-85.

[39] Harsh, 412, believes that Philoctetes should see that the bow is bigger
than he is and is destined for great things. "Heracles," he says, "made
civilization possible by achieving man's mastery over the beast and civilized
man's superiority over the barbarian." The bow, his weapon, symbolizes all
this. See also Knox [above, note 20], 140; Musurillo [above, note 21], 121;
Alt, 171-72. For a discussion of this idea see below, p. 22.

[40] Frye [above, note 5], 34.

he becomes aware of the presence of the other men, he is heard crying aloud at the pain of his hurt and the excruciating difficulty of his struggles to move (201-18). His suffering is not merely physical. Emphasis is placed on his loneliness and isolation (see 169-72, 280-82, *et passim*),[41] and the bare adequacy of his resources; only with constant desperate effort can he maintain a hold on the edge of life (273-75, 285-99). The effect of these sufferings has been to rob him of all pride. Within the first few lines that he speaks to Neoptolemus he begs for pity in his friendless, desolate torment (227-29). He pleads abjectly to Neoptolemus to take him home, or if he cannot be bothered to do that, at least to take him as far as Euboea (468-506). As I mentioned above he is aware that his odor is offensive to other men, and he is anxious for it to cause the least annoyance possible on the voyage (481-83). He is sensitive about the odor because in the past he has begged other chance visitors to the island to take him home, but they have refused, contenting

---

[41] So much has been written about the "isolation" of the Sophoclean hero that it seems necessary at this point to emphasize, what should be obvious, that the following two typical remarks are not in any way descriptive of the situation of Philoctetes, the loneliest of Sophoclean heroes:
"The consequence of [the hero's] intransigence is that isolation which has so often been described as the mark of the Sophoclean hero (Knox, 32)."
"Human greatness is of such a nature, the poet seems to have realized, that it simply cannot exist without being lonely (Opstelten [above, note 11], 191)."
The observation of W. Schadewaldt [above, note 1], 244, that the Sophoclean hero becomes more himself through suffering (see below p. 37) is equally inappropriate to Philoctetes. Philoctetes is not isolated by his own greatness, but by forces outside his own control. And his suffering is far more a debasing than a refining and exalting process.
The only writer who has appreciated the extent of Philoctetes' degradation is Jan Kott, in a very recent book on Greek tragedy, *The Eating of the Gods* (New York 1970-73), which came into my hands only when this manuscript was in the last stage of correction before printing. Kott says, 169, that, "Philoctetes is thrown to the very bottom of the human condition." However, Kott's view of the play as a whole is not at all clear, for his strange, often irritatingly elusive essay on *Philoctetes* is not really a literary analysis at all, but an appreciation written from the point of view of an existentialist and a man who experienced the horrors of World War II. Thus his belief that Philoctetes is brought very low is difficult to correlate with his emphasis, 168-69 *et passim*, on Philoctetes' being a special person, chosen by the gods. The seeming conflict of ideas is to be explained, I think, by the fact that Kott would not accept the distinction, which I put forward, between high tragedy and tragedy belonging to the ironic mode. To Kott all tragic heroes are victims, all prisoners of the human condition. So Prometheus, 35-42, is as helpless as Philoctetes, his seeming freedom of choice a delusion, his suffering ultimately meaningless.

themselves with a few words of pity and a little charity for which he has had to be grateful (305-11). He has sent messages by these men in the past, but they have had no effect, and he suspects that the travelers have not considered him worth the trouble even to do this much (494-99). Philoctetes is a man who has been maimed spiritually as well as physically. He is, like Lear, a ruin'd piece of nature.

Whether Aristotle was right in his insistence that tragedy must be moral, at least it is important to see that the plot of this play —by whatever name it may be called—is immoral. In this alone of Sophocles' dramas there is an outright villain, a persecutor (who is not, to be sure, responsible for all of Philoctetes' woes), and an innocent victim. The action of the play is a gradual revelation of the cruelties suffered by Philoctetes in the past, and in the present a progressive intensification of his torment. It may be—a thing which I doubt—that the *deus ex machina* reverses the movement and cancels out the previous disregard of Philoctetes' good. But the peculiar thing about this play is that, at least until the last scene, it almost entirely ignores the good that may come, to Philoctetes or to others, of his going to Troy and concentrates instead upon the wrong being done him by Odysseus' ruthlessness and on the cruelties endured by him in the past. He has wandered by accident into the precinct of the goddess Chryse and has been bitten by a snake which is the goddess' avatar. Because of his smell and the annoyance of his cries of anguish he has lost his right to associate with others, and is deserted by his fellows. In the extremity of his necessity he loses much of his sense of equality with others. This progressive accumulation of woes might be viewed as a process of stripping away of his physical and mental resources. He loses first his health, then his security as a member of society, then his sense of dignity as a man among men. And this process of stripping continues into the present, until the dramatic turning-point late in the play when Neoptolemus takes back the bow from Odysseus and returns it to Philoctetes. For surely it is obvious that Odysseus' trickery with which he acquires the bow is of a piece with his deceitful abandonment of Philoctetes ten years before.

Up to line 895, when Neoptolemus decides that he must abandon deceit and tell Philoctetes the truth, much of the play is devoted to a disclosure of the details of this suffering that Philoctetes previously has endured and his anger at the injustice of it: how he was bitten by Chryse and abandoned, the appearance of his cave, his struggles to sustain life, his hatred of Odysseus and the Atreidae, etc. *Philoctetes* is not a past-tense narrative, however, but a work of drama; all the while before the eyes of the audience is a reminder of the present occasion: Neoptolemus, whose intention is to deceive. Gradually this present occasion is brought into focus with the past. Partly, especially early in the play, this is by implication only, as when we learn from Philoctetes that it was by trickery and stealth that Odysseus abandoned him (268-75). The visit of the false merchant (542-627), however, makes explicit the fact that Odysseus is as callous in his rescue of Philoctetes, and as unconcerned about Philoctetes' wishes, as he was when he deserted him. The merchant-scene is one of two scenes (the other is the attack of the disease that strikes Philoctetes) that have worried critics because they have seemed episodic and unmotivated. They seem so only if the plot is regarded as a plot of intrigue. The merchant's visit does not further the goal of tricking Philoctetes into setting sail with Neoptolemus. We should not therefore waste time trying to imagine what Odysseus expected the merchant to accomplish. At this point in the play (or at any other for that matter) the audience is interested not in what is going on in Odysseus' mind but in the depth of Philoctetes' emotion. The purpose of the scene is to warn Philoctetes that Odysseus is more than just the perpetrator of an old wrong: he is a present threat. The merchant tells Philoctetes three-quarters of the truth: that the gods have proclaimed that it is necessary for the Greeks to bring him to Troy and that Odysseus has boasted, at the wager of his own head, that he will accomplish this (614-19). The function of the merchant is to inform Philoctetes that Odysseus has sworn to return Philoctetes to the Greeks will he nill he like a piece of chattel goods, in order that Neoptolemus, and we, may see what this mission of his looks like from Philoctetes' perspective. When Neoptolemus began his effort to insinuate himself into Philoctetes' graces he told himself that all of Philoctetes' torment was in the past (191-200). Now Neoptolemus is forced to face squarely the fact of Philoctetes' adamant opposition to his present intentions. Philoctetes predictably regards this as one more act of persecution. It will be another humiliation, to be brought back by Odysseus and exhibited among the Greeks (630). From this point Philoctetes' enmity no longer is a generalized thing, related to ills suffered long ago; and Neoptolemus, as his final decision to consent to do Philoctetes' will shows, now finds it impossible casually to rationalize the machinations against Philoctetes on the grounds that it is all in Philoctetes' own best interests. The sudden attack of Philoctetes' disease (732-826) serves much the same function as the news told by the merchant. It brings home to the audience and to Neoptolemus the enormity of what Philoctetes has been suffering. His physical torture is as great as that of a victim on the rack. Surely a man who has endured so much, whose wishes have been so often thwarted, should not have imposed on him any new hurt, of body or spirit.

But the hurt and the degradation are going on in the present, which emerges clearly as a continuation of the past. As I have said above, Philoctetes has felt before the disregard of other visitors to the island. Now the disingenuous claim of Neoptolemus not to know of him makes him feel that he has lost even his identity in the world, that he has become the forgotten man. His awesome sufferings to other men are not worth even the trouble of mention (254-56):

> ὦ πόλλ' ἐγὼ μοχθηρός, ὦ πικρὸς θεοῖς,
> οὗ μηδὲ κληδὼν ὧδ' ἔχοντος οἴκαδε
> μηδ' Ἑλλάδος γῆς μηδαμοῖ διῆλθέ που.

How different from the Oedipus of *Oedipus Tyrannus* who uses the first person pronoun seventeen times in his first speech. But worse than neglect, Philoctetes is forced to endure the insults of the man he hates most in the world, who thinks him hardly worth the bother of addressing (πόλλ' ἂν λέγειν ἔχοιμι πρὸς τὰ τοῦδ' ἔπη, / εἴ μοι παρείκοι, 1047-48). Finally he must watch that man walk away, the master of his bow (1054-69). And when in the face of Odysseus' insolence he attempts to jump off the cliff he is denied even the dignity of suicide (1001-1003).

Odysseus' taking of the bow has been another critical problem. There has been endless discussion about the precise wording of the oracle, whether Odysseus understands it properly or not, and the intention of Odysseus' strategem. When Philoctetes falls asleep after his attack of illness Neoptolemus refuses to leave without him, saying that the god ordered that he be brought, not just his bow (839-41). Odysseus, on the other hand, never speaks of anything but the bow, and when he walks away with it he says that either he or Teucer can wield it successfully. Is Odysseus in his egotistical self-assurance guilty of a rank misinterpretation of the oracle? [42] Or does Odysseus in reality understand that Philoctetes must come with the bow and be persuaded, and is he merely resorting to a kind of "Melian persuasion?" [43] Speculations of this sort ultimately are fruitless, for the play gives us no evidence of exactly what is going on in Odysseus' mind. It does not do so obviously because Sophocles does not think that it is important to know. But more than that, these speculations betray a lack of critical perspective. They result from a confusion of real life with what Susanne Langer calls the "virtual life" of an artistic creation.[44] When Odysseus walks off with the bow, he does not think anything because he is not a real person; the artistic conception "Odysseus" does not think anything because we are given no hint of what it may be. And the reason we are given no hint is that Odysseus' strategem is of no interest at this time. The audience at this point in the play is seeing things through the eyes of Philoctetes, who is as articulate as Odysseus is laconic, and whose feelings are as clear as Odysseus' intentions are obscure. The audience is not speculating about why Odysseus acts as he does, but is feeling outrage and despair with Philoctetes. It is saying to itself, "Even this ..."

Schlesinger is near to the truth of the reason for Odysseus' taking the bow when he says that, to the world of political machination which Odysseus represents, a man does not mean much more than a tool.[45] To Odysseus Philoctetes the man has no more intrinsic value than the bow. And by Odysseus' treatment of him Philoctetes is reduced to the status of a thing, an inanimate object, to be discarded or retrieved at will. Odysseus is almost right, too. Philoctetes has been so degraded by his evils, stripped so naked of his physical defences and his self-respect, that if he is more than a thing, he is less than a peer of men.

[42] Bowra, 267; Diller [above, note 19], 20-21.

[43] Alt [above, note 15], 148, 165; Schlesinger [above, note 20], 118, 123; A. E. Hinds, "The Prophecy of Helenus in Sophocles' *Philoctetes*," *CQ* n.s.17 (1967), 177-78.

[44] Susanne K. Langer, *Feeling and Form* (New York 1953), 212-14, 245.

[45] Schlesinger, 119. See also Linforth [above, note 16], 103-05. Odysseus' concentration on the bow, says Linforth, is a means of characterizing Odysseus and emphasizes his concern for the impersonal instrument and his disregard of the man.

I mentioned above (note 39) that certain critics emphasize the importance of the divine associations of the bow, and believe that Philoctetes is derelict in his refusal to serve the bow's greater destiny. Perhaps it is enough to say that there is no evidence whatever for this idea in the play itself. At no time in the play does anyone say or even hint that the bow is an instrument of the powers of Good to which it is Philoctetes' duty to humble himself. (I postpone until later the question, which is seriously posed in the play [see below, pp. 44-48], whether Philoctetes' going to Troy will in fact represent the triumph of good over evil.) In fact, this sounds like an idea more at home in Germanic saga or medieval knights-tales than in Greek literature. The proposition that an inanimate object, however divine its associations, is more important than a man is at the farthest remove from what might be expected of Sophocles. Moreover, if it is true, as I have argued, that the emphasis of this play is upon the torments suffered by Philoctetes, it should then be clear what this idea implies: the moral of this play must be that no suffering of an individual, no matter how excruciating, and no injustice are of any consequence when there arises the question of service to a higher good. Critics of this persuasion, no matter how much they may dislike Odysseus, must admit that it is reasonable for him to concentrate on the bow and to ignore Philoctetes' feelings about the past. I submit that this is psychologically implausible. The play makes every effort to arouse in its audience feelings of pity for Philoctetes and outrage at his suffering. To expect them to suppress these feelings and to look with satisfaction to the triumph of a cause would require an effort to convince them of the cause's importance. This the play does not do. It does not celebrate the glory of some *Aeneid*-like holy mission. If it celebrates anything, it is the importance of a small man's sufferings and his claim to a minimum of self-respect even when this claim stands in conflict with the progress of history.

Whatever transcendant good the bow may represent to Odysseus, to Philoctetes it is his sole tenuous hold on life. It has been his sole companion during his long exile (when it has been taken from him he addresses it as a loved companion, 1128-39) and his only source of sustenance. He identifies his very existence with it. When he is won over to friendship with Neoptolemus his ultimate gesture of trust is to surrender to him the bow (762-73; see also 662-70). And when Odysseus has disdainfully taken it from him, he says, ἔτ' οὐδέν εἰμι (1217; see also 1030). Philoctetes' degradation has gone virtually as far as it can. He is reduced to begging the chorus who have betrayed him to stay only a little longer (1181-85, 1190). Yet when the chorus advises him in friendship (1121, 1163-64) to yield to Odysseus and fate, he answers, Never, not even if Zeus should strike me with his thunderbolt (1197-99). Something in him is not quite defeated.

* *
*

Persecution presupposes a persecutor or persecutors. Among the emotions produced by high tragedy, which Aristotle rather inadequately describes as pity and fear, are included admiration and awe at the excellence of the hero. This admiration brings with it a sense of fulfillment or satisfaction; it is a compensating factor which helps to drive out the demon of the negative emotions, and contributes not a little to what Aristotle calls tragedy's cathartic effect. In a work whose action is primarily directed toward the persecution of a relatively innocent person this satisfaction does not come. The audience feels something like anguish and frustration (along with pity and fear), as well as anger toward the persecutors. Odysseus bears the brunt of this anger in *Philoctetes*.

This type of plot lends itself very well to political propaganda and a particularly biting kind of social criticism. Kitto tries to limit *Philoctetes* entirely to such social criticism,[46] and others have seen in this the major burden of the play's meaning. Odysseus' sophistic attributes are so obvious that it is needless to discuss them, and the relevance of his character to contemporary political and social conditions is inescapable. Jameson's observation is typical: "Sophocles, the recent victim along with much of his audience of a great deception [by the 400 oligarchs], produce[d] a play whose major interest is in the moral and psychological implications . . . of the initial deception, the conscious, carefully underlined sacrifice of values to expedience." [47] More specifically Harsh sees in the play the three main character-types discerned by Thucydides in the Peloponnesian War: Odysseus stands for success by treachery, Philoctetes for lust for revenge, Neoptolemus for the ancient

---

[46] Kitto [above, note 17], 136.
[47] M. H. Jameson, "Politics and the *Philoctetes*," *CP* 51 (1956), 219. See Jameson's article for a brief review of attempts to give contemporary political significance to this play.

simplicity in which honor so largely entered, which was laughed down and disappeared. Charles Fuqua, while he avoids allegorizing the characters of the play, perhaps goes further in emphasizing the importance of the attack on sophistry, asserting that there is an organizational antithesis in the play between φύσις, Neoptolemus' special word, and νόμος.[48]

To be sure, social criticism is an important element in the play, but for several reasons I think that the play is much more than an attack on the decadent mores of "modern" man. If it were only this the play essentially would be no more than a melodrama, with Odysseus, the representative of modern vices, the villain. (1) In the first place, Odysseus is by no means the sole object of the frustrated anger which I have described as one of the play's effects. (2) Odysseus is on the side of the gods. (3) Although the moral conflict as it is stated in the prologue is between "modern" deceitfulness represented by Odysseus and honorable directness of action, or the "ancient simplicity" represented by Neoptolemus, during the course of the play Neoptolemus' moral horizons broaden and he becomes concerned not merely about deceit, but about the larger question of justice; not just about Odysseus' dishonorable means, but about the purpose itself of the mission—which is not of Odysseus' authorship.

In support of (1) it is necessary only to point out that Odysseus is not the agent of much of the wrong about which the play complains: Philoctetes' physical suffering; the fact that just men seem to suffer and unjust men to prosper; the necessity for Philoctetes to serve the interests of and to associate with men whom he considers to be evil. In fact, Odysseus is kept carefully in the background. If Sophocles had wanted the audience to be preoccupied with Odysseus' personal villainy he need only have brought him on stage for half as long as Neoptolemus, so that he might implement his own stratagem and, so to speak, twirl his mustaches. Instead his role is so understated that some critics—I think ludi-

---

[48] Harsh [above, note 34], 409. Charles J. Fuqua, *The Thematic Structure of Sophocles' "Philoctetes,"* unpub. diss. Cornell Univ. 1964, 60, 68-72. Bowra, 286, compares Odysseus' ruthless pursuit of success with that of the Athenians in the Melian dialogue. To Reinhardt [above, note 29], 180-85, the concept of heroism in this play is colored by the spirit of the last third of the Peloponnesian War: "Der Trug ist herrschend, und nicht nur Odysseus ist der Falsche (p. 181)." (That is, even Neoptolemus starts out with a false concept of heroism, in which glory is more important than the deed itself.)

crously—have been tempted even to find something attractive and sympathetic in him.[49]

(2) I have asserted that Odysseus is on the side of the gods. In his short scene of confrontation with Philoctetes Odysseus claims to be the servant of Zeus (989-90). Not many lines later the chorus verifies this, saying in effect, It was not our trickery that overcame you but the will of the gods (1116-19). Occasionally it is claimed that these statements are false and merely self-serving,[50] but most critics (usually with distaste) accept them at face value, and the facts of the play speak for themselves. We are told by the false merchant (603-21) and later by Neoptolemus (1324-47) that Odysseus' purpose was ordained by the gods, and this is implicit in the very fact of the mission, since the mission can have no other motivation than the gods' oracle. Of course, it does not necessarily follow that the gods approve of Odysseus' methods just because it is Odysseus' intention to do their will. Those who wish to dissociate the gods from Odysseus emphasize the difference in method proposed by Odysseus and the gods. The argument runs like this: the gods and Odysseus desire the same end—to take Philoctetes to Troy. But the gods have a concern for Philoctetes' self-respect and order that he be persuaded to return to the Greek army, not tricked. Odysseus misunderstands the oracle, or perhaps tries to second-guess the gods, but he is not allowed to succeed in his ruthless purpose. And at this point in the argument solemn and lengthy pronouncements are made about the inadequacy of human understanding.[51]

I think that it is possible that we are supposed to understand that Odysseus' callous disregard of Philoctetes' wishes is contrary to the will of the gods. However, it should be seen that the gods themselves do nothing either to forestall or to repudiate Odysseus' actions. This is done by a man, who, if he is moved to do it by any wish to obey the gods, conspicuously fails to say so, giving as a reason for his action only a concern for honor and justice (1224-51).[52] In any case, the whole argument for Odysseus' misunder-

[49] Muth [above, note 23], 652-55; Méautis [above, note 30], 61, 87-90; Maddalena [above, note 23], 255-56.

[50] Kitto [above, note 17], 122-23, says that when Odysseus says this the audience does not believe him. Harsh, 410, says that the gods do not choose Odysseus as their helper, but that Odysseus unscrupulously adopts a just cause and tries to exploit it.

[51] See, for instance, Bowra, 267-69; Diller [above, note 19], 20-21, 25-27; Reinhardt, 200-201; Maddalena, 262-65.

[52] However, Adams [above, note 22], 18, believes that any magnanimous

standing the gods' will is based ultimately on just two words and
the critics' solicitude for the gods' reputation. In line 612 the false
merchant says that the gods have decreed that the Greeks will not
take Troy unless they fetch Philoctetes, πείσαντες λόγῳ. Now the
word πείθειν does not in itself preclude guile. And, as A. E. Hinds
has pointed out, in this merchant-scene it is force with which persuasion is contrasted, not guile (593-94, 618).[53] Odysseus, be it
noted, carefully avoids force. There is nowhere in the play, then,
much evidence that the gods object to Odysseus' methods, and
it surely is special pleading to argue that the inadequacy of human
understanding is one of the play's primary messages.

The irony sometimes has been remarked upon that the deceitful,
unscrupulous Odysseus tries to do the gods' will, while the upright
Philoctetes opposes it.[54] But there is an irony much deeper and
more bitter than this: that the gods have imposed horrible suffering
on Philoctetes, but for Odysseus have prospered all his ways. It is
wrong and unnecessary to attribute to the plan or will of the
gods Odysseus' gratuitous disdain of Philoctetes' feelings; it is
disturbing enough to observe that they show no disapprobation
of Odysseus' ruthlessness. In spite of Odysseus' past and present
cruelties, the gods' plan coincides precisely with his interests
and those of the hated Atreidae.[55] As Philoctetes says (446-

---

act is *ipso facto* evidence of divine inspiration: "If we look clearly at the
Sophoclean portraitures of men and women we must realize that the gods
work through the noblest instincts of these people. Everyone who reads these
plays must bear in mind that all-important fact: what is best in men and
women is used by heaven for the furtherance of its desires." I feel no compulsion to think any such thing, and there is not the smallest shred of evidence
in the play that Neoptolemus is inspired by the gods to return the bow. On
the contrary, Neoptolemus' sermon immediately after he does so, about the
necessity for men to yield to the gods (1314-23), indicates clearly that he
realizes that his action has jeopardized the accomplishment of the gods' will.

[53] Hinds [above, note 43], 179. However, once earlier in the play the word
πείθειν is used where it clearly refers to artless persuasion. Odysseus says
in the prologue (103) that πείθειν will not work on Philoctetes; so that when
the words of the oracle contradict him this should be noticed by the audience.

[54] See Kirkwood [above, note 2], 262; Reinhardt, 176.

[55] However, Kitto [above, note 17], 137: "The play is a Comedy in the
sense that wickedness is punished and virtue triumphs." Then Kitto admits
that the wicked triumph too but asserts that the audience does not feel this
(see above, p. 8 and note 18). But how can the audience' feeling fail to be
influenced by its rational understanding of the facts of the play? Kitto
emphasizes that the audience is witness to the confounding of Odysseus.
But the fact is that there are two reversals: first Odysseus is frustrated, then
when Philoctetes is about to be granted his wish to be taken home a *deus ex
machina* puts him right back on the boat with Odysseus.

47), οὐδέν πω κακόν γ᾽ ἀπώλετο, / ἀλλ᾽ εὖ περιστέλλουσιν αὐτὰ δαίμονες.

(3) A third reason to believe that the play is more than a piece of social or political criticism is that during the course of the play Neoptolemus finds far more to arouse his moral concern than just the knavery of man.

We are told by Dio Chrysostom (52.15) that the introduction of Neoptolemus into the story of Philoctetes' return to the Greeks is Sophocles' own invention. Since Sophocles did invent Neoptolemus' presence on Odysseus' expedition he must have intended it to serve a definite artistic purpose, and a comparison of this play with what Dio tells us of the earlier versions of Aeschylus and Euripides makes it reasonably certain what that purpose was. Neoptolemus was not invented to fill a role of intermediary which was demanded by the received plot, for there was no such role in the earlier plays. Dio tells us (52.14) that Aeschylus' Odysseus arrived on Lemnos unaccompanied, and that Euripides' Odysseus was accompanied by Diomedes. Whatever Diomedes' function may have been, it was not to act as an intermediary for Odysseus, since Dio tells us that Euripides' Odysseus was disguised so as not to be recognized. In any case Diomedes would have been very inadequate for the role, linked by tradition as he is with Odysseus in character as well as in adventure. (As in this play; see lines 416-18, where Philoctetes says, But the offspring of Tydeus and the son of Sisyphus bought by Laertes will not be dead, for they should not be alive!) What Neoptolemus brings to the play that Diomedes could not is neutrality. He stands midway between the other two characters with their strong wills and clear certainty, entirely convinced by neither. He begins the play consenting, with grave reservations, to help Odysseus; he ends consenting, again against his better judgement, to help Philoctetes. Neoptolemus comes very close to playing the mythical role of "ideal spectator." He is a young man who intends good but who has never been really tested, and whose principles are not firmly established in his own mind. Thus he can see both the right and the wrong on both sides.

It probably is significant that the chorus plays a smaller role in this than in the other extant plays of Sophocles. I have no doubt that at least part of the reason for this is that Neoptolemus has usurped its function of sympathizer and confidant. And he provides a much more satisfactory measure of, and commentary upon, the goodness and highmindedness of the hero than could the usual Greek chorus of feckless and fearful commoners, slave girls, or old men. In most Greek tragedies the chorus is debarred from action on the hero's exalted level, and to a greater or lesser degree the ethic of all choruses is the prudent one of the common man. The typical chorus provides a balance against the hero's extremism because it can see two sides to every question: the realistically practical as well as the noble. Neoptolemus shares this ability, but for a different reason (for, unlike a chorus, he is ambitious): that his moral character as yet is not entirely formed. However, he has a natural inclination to goodness (see, for instance, 79-80, 88-89, and 94-95). And as the son of Achilles he represents a much higher standard of ἀρετή than any chorus could. He has none of a chorus' overriding concern for prudence; he is moved by the same abstract sense of honor that enables Philoctetes to stand firm against Odysseus. In fact, he is induced to undertake the deception of Philoctetes by the prospect of future honor. But at the beginning his conception of the nature of honor still is unclear. He confuses it with fame, and rather uncomfortably allows himself to be persuaded that honor can coexist with shame. Thus he consents to do a deal with necessity—until Philoctetes' perseverance brings him to reject τὸ αἰσχρόν. Unlike a chorus, whose initiative is limited by its weakness and caution, he can act; that he fails through most of the play to take any decisive action is due to uncertainty rather than to weakness. And that he ultimately moves from Odysseus' side to Philoctetes' cannot be without significance.

In the prologue Neoptolemus does not question that Odysseus' purpose (as opposed to his methods), to take Philoctetes to Troy, is a good one. In fact, one can hardly see how he could question it, for he is told that Philoctetes' arrival at Troy will bring relief to the Greek army and is ordained by fate. But more, it will bring glory to Neoptolemus himself, since he will share in Troy's conquest. As Alt says, how could the son of Achilles fail to be responsive to the promise of honor?[56] Nevertheless, Neoptolemus' agreement is not without qualms. He is troubled by the doubt, which he suppresses for the time, that Odysseus' dishonorable methods will fatally compromise the honor that he hopes to attain. It has to be argued by those who interpret this as a political play

---

[56] Alt [above, note 15], 148.

that Neoptolemus' outlook does not essentially change in the course
of the play, and that his better feelings, which are so visible in
the prologue, merely come again to the surface. The argument must
be, in other words, that he finally is overcome by scruples about
Odysseus' methods only, and not by misgivings about the expedition's purpose, and he returns the bow simply because he has
obtained it dishonestly. This is a plausible argument, for in the
course of the play Neoptolemus certainly does not reject honor
as a good; in fact, when he takes the bow back from Odysseus the
first reason he gives for doing so is that he worsted Philoctetes
ἀπάταισιν αἰσχραῖς ... καὶ δόλοις (1228).

However, there is a gap in this interpretation. Neoptolemus may
believe that ensnaring Philoctetes by trickery is dishonorable, but
in the prologue he is very far from doubting that it is a good thing.
Moreover, before he returns the bow he already has abandoned
deceit so far as it is possible for him to do so. He has found that he
is unable to take Philoctetes on board ship without telling him
the truth. So he does so (915-16), abandoning the method but not
the purpose, for at this point he intends Philoctetes to come with
him against his will. He tries being honest with Philoctetes and
finds that this is not enough to allay his qualms. Therefore, some
new factor has entered during the course of the play to influence
his decision to return the bow. In his argument with Odysseus,
just a few lines further on, he tells what it is. He repeats (1234),
I have obtained the bow αἰσχρῶς, then adds, κοὐ δίκῃ. (This is in
direct contradiction of his uneasy protest to the angry Philoctetes
earlier in line 926 that he must keep the bow, distasteful as it is to
him, because justice compels him to do so: τό τ' ἔνδικόν με καὶ τὸ
συμφέρον ποιεῖ). The possibility that Neoptolemus comes to regard
his mission as unjust is unthinkable, of course, the mission being
associated as it is with the will of the gods. So that critics seemingly
have given these words a very narrow interpretation, for no one
has thought them worth much discussion. Consequently, Neoptolemus' motive for returning the bow has given critics great trouble.

The usual way out of the difficulty has been to assert that
Neoptolemus becomes more concerned not about justice but about
the gods' will. He comes to realize that the strategy of the mission
has been wrongly conceived because the gods want Philoctetes to
return to the Greeks willingly. If this is so Neoptolemus is re-
markably reticent about saying it. He does not give as a reason

for his decision to return the bow, The gods do not want me to
do this, but, It is shameful and unjust to do this. And the only
information about the gods' will that Neoptolemus receives during
the play which could lead him to this decision is contained in one
phrase, which I discussed above (p. 26), πείσαντες λόγῳ (612),
occurring long before Neoptolemus repudiates Odysseus.[57] There-
after the need to persuade Philoctetes never is mentioned again,
and if Sophocles wants us to believe that Neoptolemus' primary
motive is to do the gods' will, his failure to develop the idea is
inexplicable.[58] But if we overlook the lack of evidence that Neoptolemus' return of the bow is a pious act, there is nevertheless
evidence in the play that actually contradicts the idea.

After Neoptolemus returns the bow he is persuaded to go yet one
step further, and consents to take Philoctetes home. Even if
Neoptolemus believes that the gods do not want Philoctetes to
be forced by Odysseus' methods to go to Troy, he still most assuredly
believes that the gods want Philoctetes to go to Troy. He tells us
this precisely and at length after he returns Philoctetes' bow to
him (1314-42). But he then consents to take Philoctetes in the
opposite direction, to abet him in deliberate disobedience of the
gods' will. There has been a strong critical tendency to disregard
entirely Neoptolemus' consent to take Philoctetes back home as a
separate decision from his decision to give back the bow; or at
best to consider it a kind of unconsidered reflex of the frustration
of failing in his mission.[59] Many critics talk rather vaguely of

---

[57] D. B. Robinson, "Topics in Sophocles' *Philoctetes*," *CQ* n.s. 19 (1969),
47, points out that Greek oracles are notoriously unclear. Even when their end
is clear the method of achieving that fulfillment often is a difficult problem.
So that Odysseus' adoption of deceit in the service of persuasion is not in the
circumstances unreasonable, and Neoptolemus has no way of suddenly being
sure that Odysseus' way is not consistent with the oracle. The truth is that
Neoptolemus is moved to return the bow by moral rather than religious
considerations. As Robinson, 51, says, "Neoptolemus' virtue is something
more than fidelity to oracles, Odysseus' vice is worse than neglect of oracles."

[58] What certain critics lack in evidence, however, they make up for in
rhetoric. Bowra, writing in 1944, drags up the red herring of the problem of
the moral conflict between obedience to a military superior and obedience to
moral right. When Neoptolemus finally returns the bow this, he asserts, 298,
is disobedience to Odysseus but "obedience to the gods." See also Adams
[above, note 22], 154; Schlesinger [above, note 20], 118; Knox [above, note
20], 118-20.

[59] Bowra, 300, calls it an attempt to do "the second-best" thing, ignoring
the fact that it excludes the possibility of the fulfillment in the future of the
gods' will.

nobility and honor. "Neoptolemus," says Harsh, "finally agrees to take Philoctetes home not because he thinks that this is the right course, but merely because he is pressed so hard on a point of personal honor." [60] This will not work, for Greek honor is not mere *machismo*. However illogically a Greek hero may ignore practicality in his pursuit of a goal which he knows is not attainable, he never overlooks moral logic. His rigidity inevitably is based on a firm belief in the correctness of his course of action. When Neoptolemus consents to take Philoctetes home it is an act of great audacity, and he does it because he thinks it is the right thing to do. But he does not think that it is what the gods want. Any complete and consistent interpretation of the play must reconcile this contradiction.

At the beginning of the play Neoptolemus' willingness to do what the gods' oracle has ordained is unequivocal. In the prologue he is troubled by Odysseus' proposal. But as is to be expected of a young man and a son of Achilles, he is preoccupied with considerations of heroic honor; so that he is disturbed—at least consciously—only by the slyness of Odysseus' methods. It is not my nature, he says, to accomplish anything ἐκ τέχνης κακῆς (88). Moreover, he asserts (94-95), I would rather fail καλῶς δρῶν than be victorious κακῶς. However, at this point his own morality is a very simplistic one indeed. If you use overt, direct action to get what you want, then it is honest. He is willing, he says, to take Philoctetes πρὸς βίαν but μὴ δόλοισιν (90-91). And he adds naively (91-92), With only one foot he won't be able to best so many of us. It is difficult to believe that Sophocles did not intend, even this early in the play, to provoke a certain uneasiness about the justice of making Philoctetes go to Troy; to plant in the minds of his audience an unspoken doubt, Is the use of force, however καλόν, really more decent?

However, Neoptolemus soon shows that his moral sensibility is much finer than this. The reality of Philoctetes' torment confronts him with the bewildering fact that punishment may be visited upon an innocent man without cause. Happiness may not follow immediately on the footsteps of honesty, and there may not be a direct relationship between guilt and suffering. In his perplexity he rationalizes (191-200):

---

[60] Harsh [above, note 34], 411.

> This doesn't surprise me. These sufferings are from the gods
> (θεῖα) and came upon him from savage Chryse. And surely
> what he now bears he bears by the plan of one of the gods,
> so that he may not stretch his divine arrows against Troy
> before the time comes when Troy is fated to be conquered
> by them.

Surprisingly, this specious apology often is taken at face value.
"Questo è il senso religioso della tragedia," says Perrotta.[61] The
tragedy must therefore make little sense, for these lines do not
solve any problem of cosmic or divine injustice. If they are true,
this means that the gods must be not only callously brutal but
clumsy and incompetent, who have to make a man suffer for nearly
ten years as Philoctetes has in order to get him to Troy at the
proper moment.[62] This explanation so clearly is desperately inadequate that, far from allaying any suspicions that the audience
may have conceived about the gods' culpability, it rather calls the
audience' attention to the question. The question of the gods' share
of responsibility—whether the gods are good or bad in a world in
which this kind of suffering can happen—might perfectly well have
been avoided, as it is in *Oedipus Tyrannus*. Instead, Sophocles
voluntarily brings it forward near the beginning of the play.
Neoptolemus reminds us not only that a divinity, Chryse, caused
Philoctetes' wound but also that the gods have allowed him to
suffer in lonely isolation for so many years without intervening,
and suggests gratuitously that this has been in furtherance of some
active intention. After this it seems to me that any spectator or
reader must be conscious of the gods' role in the events with which
the play is concerned; and that he must at the end be consciously
satisfied or dissatisfied with the gods' dispensation in accordance
with his interpretation of these events.

Kitto, as he would, sees the trap and denies that this is so.
This problem, he says, is "... the most profound of problems, the
problem of suffering and Divine Providence. Once raised, this
problem must dominate the play. But it does not: it drops stone-
dead." He then explains that Sophocles did not intend to raise the

---

[61] Perrotta [above, note 23], 414. Bowra, 290, rather desperately takes
refuge in a legalistic theology: "Philoctetes has not sinned deliberately
against the gods, but he has to suffer for breaking their rules."

[62] Kitto [above, note 17], 112. See also Linforth [above, note 16], 107-08.

question at all; that Neoptolemus merely is expressing his own disturbance about his mission. "He dislikes the idea that the men he is now serving are a set of unconscionable villains, and therefore he blames the gods—as many other characters do in Greek tragedy, always wrongly." [63] "Always wrongly" is a revealing phrase. I leave aside the fact that it is untrue, as Kitto himself would admit in a less heated moment. It betrays the *a priori* reasoning that so often surfaces in critical treatments of *Philoctetes*: Sophocles believes that the gods are good, therefore Sophocles cannot question the goodness of the gods.[64] Kitto says that Neoptolemus desperately blames the gods for something that they did not do. But this is just not so: τὰ παθήματα κεῖνα πρὸς αὐτὸν / τῆς ὠμόφρονος Χρύσης ἐπέβη, says Neoptolemus (193-94), which is the simple truth. It is true that men are partly to blame for Philoctetes' past sufferings; this play is no mere anti-religious treatise. But the gods bear a share of this responsibility, too, and the playwright takes care to draw this to our attention.[65] Moreover, it is even more wrong to say as Kitto

---

[63] Kitto, 112.

[64] To so many critics the benignity of the gods in Sophocles is simply axiomatic and requires no further demonstration. Schlesinger [above, note 20], 103, asserting like Kitto that it is not the gods but men who are wrong, is representative (here he is discussing the fact that Odysseus' plan comes to grief): "Es ist höchst unwahrscheinlich, dass Sophokles die Götter den Menschen etwas Unmögliches anbefehlen lässt. Nicht die göttliche Forderung ist absurd, sondern das was die Menschen daraus machen...." Why is it unwahrscheinlich? Harsh, 408-409, trying to convince that the ending of the play is good and what Philoctetes really wants, goes even further: "There can be no dichotomy ... between the ideal and the real ending or the divine and the human ending. Especially for the Greeks *the divine is an extension of the human* (emphasis mine)." What does this mean? That whatever the gods do for men must be good for them? Perrotta, 422, faces much more honestly the fact that Sophocles does, indeed, call into question the good will of the gods: "Il poeta pone, non risolve, il problema della giustizia degli dèi." But this disturbs Perrotta's Catholic sensibilities very much, and he asserts, 421, by way of qualification, "Il religiosissimo Sofocle non avrebbe certo pronunziate in suo nome le parole [blasfeme] che fa dire a Filottete." I'd be curious to know how a dramatic poet could put such questions in his own name. Finally, of course, Bowra, 263: "We can hardly believe that Sophocles intended our moral feelings to run counter to what is desired by the gods." A sort of piously meaningless statement intended to cut off further questioning.

[65] Alt [above, note 15], 174, believes that, in spite of the fact that there is no ultimate justification of the way Philoctetes has suffered, simply because the gods do take part in the affairs of men this play is not so pessimistic as the late plays of Euripides, such as *Orestes* and *Iphigeneia in Aulis*, in which you seem to have a dissolution of all order. Here the gods touch the affairs of men and their will gives order to the world, so that human life is not without

does that after this the problem of the gods' justice is dropped.

The plot of this play is a queer, turned-around one. The man who in the first scene assumes the role of villain sets out to drag the hero forcibly to what the audience has every reason to believe is "the good." He is unsuccessful, and the action moves further and further away from the known end, the conclusion that the audience knows must occur. As others have remarked, the audience must have been puzzled and uneasy. The expected conclusion is Philoctetes' salvation through the gods' grace. But the advantages that are to accrue to Philoctetes are not directly referred to at all until about line 720, almost halfway through the play, when, near the end of an ode describing his woes, the chorus says, After all this he will be great (719-20). Ignoring the impending grace of the gods, the early part of the play focuses on the past, and in particular on past injustices. Immediately after Neoptolemus raises (or, if you follow Kitto, fails to raise) the question of divine justice, Philoctetes appears. He soon learns that his visitors are Greeks, but claim never to have heard of him. His immediate reaction is to complain about the gods: Oh indeed, I am wretched and hated by the gods that no news of my situation reached home .... But those who sacrilegiously cast me out can keep silent and laugh, while my disease grows ever worse (254-59). Whether Sophocles intends for us to believe him or not, at least there can be no doubt that Philoctetes in his bitterness doubts the justice of the gods.

Since his visitors seem not to know him, Philoctetes continues the conversation with an anguished description of his painful suffering, and of the way he was abandoned on the island. In these lines Neoptolemus is told how callously the Atreidae and Odysseus deserted Philoctetes, and Philoctetes' anger is directed entirely toward them. He mentions the gods only once, but then in a significant way (314-16):

---

hope. It seems to me that the fact of the gods' order is a very faint consolation if the order is not a good one. What Alt ignores is that if the gods are to be given direct credit for the good they must be held to blame for the bad. As Pratt [above, note 21], 280, puts it, in a world in which the will of the gods is immanent, the moral issue is also a religious issue. (A curiosity worth noting is that Schadewaldt [above, note 1] says almost the same thing about Sophocles that Alt says about Euripides: that the Sophoclean hero, by comparison with the Homeric, suffers much more because he is cut off from divinity, while the Homeric hero never is alone in his suffering, 240.)

τοιαῦτ' Ἀτρεῖδαί μ' ἥ τ' Ὀδυσσέως βία,
ὦ παῖ, δεδράκασ'· οἷς Ὀλύμπιοι θεοὶ
δοῖέν ποτ' αὐτοῖς ἀντίποιν' ἐμοῦ παθεῖν.

Now, the audience knows that the gods are not about to punish
Odysseus and the Atreidae but to reward them. And Philoctetes
just has prompted us to doubt what the gods are about when they
make the innocent suffer while the impious are allowed σῖγ'
ἔχοντες γελᾶν. The conversation now turns from Philoctetes'
suffering to news from Troy. Philoctetes learns that his friends
Achilles, Ajax, and Patroclus are dead; Nestor has lost his son
Antilochus. But those whom he hated or despised, Thersites, the
Atreidae, Odysseus, and Diomedes are, in Neoptolemus' words,
flourishing in the army of the Greeks (420). Finally, in his bitterness
Philoctetes blurts (446-52):

> ... Nothing evil yet has perished but the gods care for them
> well, and somehow delight in turning the villains and knaves
> away from Hades; but always they send the just and good
> from life. How am I to reconcile these things, how praise
> when, praising things divine, I find the gods evil?

So much for Kitto's assertion that the problem of divine injustice
"drops stone-dead."

At this point a plausible objection might be made to my emphasis
on the doubts expressed in the play about the gods' justice. Briefly,
this objection would be that Sophocles' gods are not unjust but
un-just, or, as Cedric Whitman has put it, "supramoral." [66] I have
tried to show that Sophocles is very far from being, as some would
have him, a defender of the faith, but this has been shown before
by people like Whitman, Kirkwood, and Schadewaldt, and it does
not mean that Sophocles takes a hostile, or even an ironic, view
of the gods. As Kirkwood says, "It is in the nature of deity, as
Sophocles portrays deity, to permit suffering; but it does not
follow that deity is cruel or unjust—the attitude that demands
that deity attend to the worldly success of the good is not the
highest type of religious thought." [67] Elsewhere in Kirkwood's book
this argument, that in Sophocles the gods are impersonal but not

---

[66] Whitman [above, note 3], 245.
[67] Kirkwood [above, note 2], 176-77.

actively malicious, is discussed in more detail, and it is expressed in clearer outline than anywhere else I know. Kirkwood shows that in various places in various plays the idea is found that, "... deity is hostile to human endeavor, and if it takes account of man at all it does so only to knock him down, for no moral reason." [68] But on the pages that follow he shows that another group of statements culled from the plays says that the gods bring both good and bad; and still a third group that the gods are helpful and bring good. [69] From this he concludes that what is expressed in the mouths of Sophocles' characters is "... the inconclusive and heterogeneous group of attitudes characteristic of the archaic age, and still widely held in fifth century Athens .... It is a religious outlook in which the constant attribute of the gods is power." [70] Kirkwood adds that the dominant feeling of this religious outlook is one of fear,[71] but he insists that this should not be accepted naïvely as Sophocles' own religious attitude, and he argues that what happens in each of the plays, viewed as a whole, contradicts this attitude; that the plays depict the gods as generally on the side of justice.[72] However, he admits that the gods "... are impersonal, remote and indifferent to human suffering." He adds, "If we find this indifference unjust, then the gods are unjust." [73]

This neutral willingness of divinity to permit human suffering, if it correctly describes Sophocles' world-view, justifies Opstelten's description of Sophocles as pessimistic, but not the assertion I made earlier in this paper that in some of his plays his attitude is negative and disillusioned (see above, pp. 5-6). Kirkwood's "indifference" is that of impersonal forces, the forces of the universe which, relentless as they are and overwhelming as they are, do not reduce the hero to nothing, but allow him to retain his personal dignity. In fact it is with these forces, or with a situation to which they contribute, that the hero's idealism finds itself in conflict, and they provide a test in which his nobility of spirit manifests itself.[74] And Kirkwood believes that the hero's devotion to an ideal is such

---

[68] Kirkwood, 265.

[69] Kirkwood, 266-67.

[70] Kirkwood, 271.

[71] Kirkwood, 272.

[72] Kirkwood, 271-79.

[73] Kirkwood, 279.

[74] Kirkwood, 177: "The ideal [of the hero] ... [is] created out of the clash of heroic character and testing situation."

a strong compensating factor that it is wrong even to call Sophocles pessimistic. Thus Schadewaldt, whose article, "Sophokles und das Leid," is in substantial agreement with Kirkwood's treatment of this question, says that in his suffering a greater "Ernst" comes over the hero and he is refined—he becomes more himself (see above, p. 6 and note 13).[75] Now, whatever can be said of Philoctetes, it cannot be said that he has been refined by his suffering. He has been so degraded by the assaults made on his health, his security, and finally his self-respect, that in his bitter desperation he can cry out to Odysseus, in essence, Why do you come here now to persecute me, ὃς οὐδέν εἰμι (1030; these words are repeated in line 1217; see above, p. 23)? To both Kirkwood and Schadewaldt the distinctive element and the subject of real interest in Sophoclean drama is not the cruelty of the forces opposing the hero but the nobility of his conduct as he meets their challenge. In *Philoctetes*, on the contrary, the emphasis is on the cruelty; Philoctetes' response is no more than passive, a dogged effort to hold on to life and to some small shred of self-respect when he has lost all else; and even in this passive resistance he is not allowed to succeed.

*　*
　*

The unspoken question asked by Neoptolemus' lame excuse for Philoctetes' past torments is, Why? If this is not an adequate reason, what *is* the meaning of it all? The same question is implicit in each of Philoctetes' complaints in the scene that follows (219-541); and it is explicit in his anguished exclamation at the climax of his tale of past woes (451-52; see above, p. 35): How can I praise the gods ... when I find them evil? The question simply hangs in the air unanswered, obviously because there is no answer: it was all meaningless. It is clear from Neoptolemus' subsequent behavior that this is the conclusion to which he comes. But if Neoptolemus is unable to justify the past, at any rate he can look with equanimity to the future when he will be instrumental in bringing to Philoctetes good in return for all the past evil.

The notion that the workings of universal forces, the gods and fate, are meaningless or beyond man's understanding is nothing new in Greek literature, of course. It is clearly to be seen both in

---

[75] Schadewaldt, 244.

Achilles' story of the urns of Zeus in book 24 of the *Iliad* and in Sophocles' *Oedipus Tyrannus*. Hans Diller has argued that a basic theme running through all of Sophoclean drama is that of the insufficiency of human understanding.[76] It does not follow, however, that because human understanding is inadequate human aspirations are blameworthy. Witness Oedipus. And Diller believes that in Sophoclean drama doubts are in fact raised about the morality of the world-order that are not removed.[77] What keeps these doubts from monopolizing attention in such a tragic situation is concentration on the human participation.[78] Heroes of such plots are given scope of action to compass or cooperate in their own destruction, as do Achilles and Oedipus. Diller clearly believes that man's inadequate understanding in Sophoclean drama is another manifestation of the human predicament of high tragedy: man reaches high in order to manipulate the divine dispensation for the realization of his own ambitions, but miscalculates and fails.[79]

In *Philoctetes*, however, I argue that the principal character is distinguished by no ambition and cannot be thought in any way to be a cause of the disasters that have befallen him; that, in fact, every human action in the play proves to be feckless. What distinguishes this play from *Oedipus Tyrannus* or *Antigone* is the element of control. Control here is almost completely out of the hands of mortals. The gods initiate the action, and in the end bring it to accomplishment. (This, incidentally, is one reason that some people feel that the play is episodic. There is little cause-and-effect relationship among events because (1) most of the human efforts in the play have no effect, or have an effect that is immediately reversed, and (2) two of the play's events have no definable cause, happening because of chance, fate, and/or divine intervention. But

---

[76] Diller [above, note 19], 20-21, says that in this play the theme is realized in Odysseus but not in Philoctetes.

[77] Diller, 10: "Im sophokleischen Drama wird das Geschehen in seiner Unertrinnbarkeit ohne Rest durchschaubar gemacht, nicht aber der Zweifel an der Gerechtigkeit oder der Moralität der Weltordnung, soweit er überhaupt ausgesprochen wird, erklärt."

[78] "Es gilt auch hier ... dass Sophokles nichts daran liegt, das Geschehen in seinen Tragödien mit menschlichen Vorstellungen von Gerechtigkeit oder Moral, sei es positiv oder negativ, zu konfrontieren. Wohl aber liegt ihm daran, die eindeutige Klarheit der göttlichen Aussage gegenüber allem menschlichen Fehlwissen darzutun (Diller, 24)."

[79] Actually, Diller believes, 25, that in the later plays the hero's presumption of adequate knowledge is more specific; but in all the plays someone believes falsely that he can act successfully on the basis of his knowledge.

this episodic quality is not necessarily due to the play's being clumsily constructed. A sense of the causelessness of events and the futility of human endeavor—a sense of being imprisoned by forces beyond one's control or even rational prediction—is also characteristic of literary phenomena like the novels of Kafka or the comedy of the absurd, which have their roots in twentieth century existentialism.) In a play like this, in which everything is in the gods' control, the audience can accept with equanimity the proposition that the gods' solicitude for man's welfare is uncertain only if it has an abiding faith in the good intentions of the divine. Otherwise it will react, with Philoctetes, with a sense of frustration at the seeming irrationality of things. Bowra, along with others, argues that the Greeks of the fifth century have this kind of confidence in the gods which, to be sure, may be seen in some authors like Aeschylus and Pindar.[80] This assertion of general faith, however, seems very doubtful to me. One could marshall an impressive array of fifth-century doubts about the existence of divine justice or of divinity at all. It seems much more likely that popular belief was characterized by an "inconclusive and heterogeneous group of attitudes" which Kirkwood finds expressed in Sophocles' plays.[81] However, in the last analysis, the willingness of critics to overlook the importance of the doubts expressed by Philoctetes in the first scene is due to their knowledge, shared by Neoptolemus, that in the end the gods are going to put it all right.

But do they in fact put it all right? Neoptolemus believes to the end that Philoctetes would be better off if he would yield to the necessity placed upon him by the gods and accept the concomitant practical benefits. But at last he consents to an act of quixotic folly

---

[80] Bowra, 285. Reinhardt [above, note 29], 200, who also believes that Philoctetes' doubts about divine justice derive from an insufficient view of things, quotes a passage from the Hippocratic *de victu* (1.11 = 22 C 1 Diels-Kranz) which contains many reminiscences of Heracleitus: "What the gods have ordered is eternally right, whether just or not." (Bowra, too, 284, quotes this passage. A similar idea is expressed in Heracleitus 22 B 102 Diels-Kranz: τῷ μὲν θεῷ καλὰ πάντα καὶ ἀγαθὰ καὶ δίκαια, ἄνθρωποι δὲ ἃ μὲν ἄδικα ὑπειλήφασιν ἃ δὲ δίκαια.) The Heracleitean author, however, as my colleague Professor L. Shannon DuBose has pointed out to me, was speaking of a metaphysical "rightness," not one that refers to human concepts of moral justice. Quotation games of this sort can cut both ways, too. Heracleitus also says, 22 B 53 Diels-Kranz: "Strife is the father of all things". See also Heracleitus 22 A 22. I am grateful to Professor DuBose for discussing Heracleitus with me and referring me to these fragments.

[81] Kirkwood, 271.

which will attempt to accomplish the opposite of the gods' wish that Philoctetes go to Troy. Why does he do this? Clearly by the end of the play Neoptolemus has become convinced that Philoctetes' going to Troy at least is not an unqualified good. I believe that it is in the merchant-scene that Neoptolemus' change of heart begins to take place.[82] In this scene one of Odysseus' men appears disguised as a merchant and tells Philoctetes that Odysseus is coming to get him and take him back to Troy. The presumed purpose is to encourage Philoctetes to sail with Neoptolemus immediately. This scene, as has often been remarked, does not further the plot, for when the merchant appears Philoctetes already is on the point of departure. But one change does take place as the result of this scene: after it Neoptolemus seems reluctant rather than eager to leave the island. Kirkwood has pointed out that just before the merchant's appearance Neoptolemus seems to think the weather favorable (466-67) and appears to be ready to sail.[83] He urges Philoctetes to come at once (526). However, a little later when Philoctetes, in alarm at the news of Odysseus, wants to leave, Neoptolemus says that they must wait because the wind is adverse (640). It has been suggested that what changes Neoptolemus' mind is the phrase I have discussed before (p. 26), πείσαντες λόγῳ in line 612. Neoptolemus is reminded or learns that Philoctetes must be brought back by persuasion.[84] But the idea is unconvincing to me that Neoptolemus is prompted to a purely intellectual decision—to a judgement that their methodology is wrong—by one phrase in the middle of a highly emotional scene. I believe that a much more fundamental change takes place: during the scene Neoptolemus' confidence is shaken that Philoctetes' return to the Greeks will effect a happy ending. Linforth is much nearer the truth when he says that the merchant's speech solidifies Philoctetes' antagonism toward Odysseus.[85] The effect of the scene is to focus Philoctetes' attention, away from the injustices of the past, onto Odysseus' present purpose. It forces Neoptolemus to face the fact of Philoctetes' opposition to a return to Troy and his outrage at the idea of cooperation with Odysseus (see above, pp. 19-20). This is why Neoptolemus hesitates to board ship and implement the fraud: the present is too uncomfortably like the past.

---

[82] As does Alt [above, note 15], 156.
[83] Kirkwood, 59.
[84] Kirkwood, 81; Adams, 147.   [85] Linforth [above, note 16], 118.

When I spoke above of Philoctetes' past suffering as meaningless, I meant that it could not be justified in terms of human morality. It happened suddenly and arbitrarily, without intelligible reason, and without regard for the man's wishes or his good. In the next scene we are shown dramatically how sudden and arbitrary, and how cruel, an attack of the disease can be. But the merchant-scene concentrates on the circumstances associated with Philoctetes' salvation, and the suspicion grows that it is to be just as meaningless as his past calamity. It is just as sudden and arbitrary. Why now after so many years? was the question nagging at Neoptolemus' brave assertion that the timing was all part of a god's plan (191-200). Now the salvation is seen to be absurdly inappropriate: Philoctetes again deceived, by the same man, whom he hates most in the world, constrained again to accept what he least wants (πεισθήσομαι γὰρ ὧδε κἀξ Ἅιδου θανὼν / πρὸς φῶς ἀνελθεῖν, 624-25).

This is why Neoptolemus hesitates to sail, and it is also the reason, when after his attack of illness Philoctetes again is able to embark, that Neoptolemus tells him the truth (915-16). He becomes convinced that Philoctetes must not again be treated like a thing; that his feelings must not again be utterly disregarded. Neoptolemus no longer defines the moral question as one of honest, direct action vs. guile. Neoptolemus, of course, does not approve of guile, but he also does not, after telling Philoctetes the truth, proceed to overpower him. He does set out tentatively to force Philoctetes to come with him but this effort is abortive and he does not return to it. Clearly he comes to the conclusion that simple honest force is not an appropriate way to deal with Philoctetes. As Pratt says, for Neoptolemus, "[t]he question of honesty has become the question of justice." [86] When later he takes the bow from Odysseus to return it to Philoctetes he says not only, I took it by treachery..., but, also, I took it οὐ δίκη (see above, p. 29). What matters to Neoptolemus now is the element of constraint, and after telling Philoctetes the truth he proceeds, until interrupted by Odysseus, to try to persuade him to come to Troy voluntarily (917-19):

---

[86] Pratt [above, note 21], 280. Other critics have seen that Neoptolemus' moral horizons widen during the course of the play. Knox [above, note 20], 138, says, "He has come to higher ideals of moral conduct than could have been expected of the boy who was averse to lying but ready to use superior force against a sick man." In the view of Maddalena, 249-51, Neoptolemus the boy morally comes of age during the course of the day.

Neoptolemus: μὴ στέναζε, πρὶν μάθῃς.
Philoctetes: ποῖον μάθημα; τί με νοεῖς δρᾶσαί ποτε;
Neoptolemus: σῶσαι κακοῦ μὲν πρῶτα τοῦδ'....

If Philoctetes is to be returned by Odysseus as he was abandoned, at least Neoptolemus does not want it to be against his will. Philoctetes must have the consideration due to him as a man. And if he can persuade Philoctetes to consent to the rational, practical course of action, Neoptolemus can still hope for a happy ending.

When Neoptolemus tells Philoctetes the truth, Philoctetes demands that the bow be returned to him. This Neoptolemus refuses to do, saying (925-26),

τῶν γὰρ ἐν τέλει κλύειν
τὸ τ' ἔνδικόν με καὶ τὸ συμφέρον ποεῖ.

The coincidence of justice and expediency is a convenient thing to believe in, of course, and among other things Neoptolemus is making one more attempt to accommodate Odysseus' cynical practicality to his own idealism. But he still can reasonably hope for this happy coincidence. For at this point it is only the circumstances surrounding his mission to which Neoptolemus objects, not its purpose. He still has two strong reasons to believe that the return of Philoctetes to the Greek army will be an act of compensatory justice: at Troy (1) Philoctetes will win glory, and (2) he will be cured.

Both of these Philoctetes rejects. Neoptolemus is quickly relieved of any delusion that the possibility of winning renown among the Greeks is a compelling argument to Philoctetes (even though, in his last attempt to persuade Philoctetes, he does again make one half-hearted reference to it, ll. 1344-47). Odysseus appears, with his abrupt, contemptuous treatment of Philoctetes providing a dramatic illustration of what troubles Neoptolemus most about this mission: the Greeks' disregard of Philoctetes' wants and his dignity. Odysseus can hardly be bothered to argue with Philoctetes (1047-48, 1052-53):

πόλλ' ἂν λέγειν ἔχοιμι πρὸς τὰ τοῦδ' ἔπη,
εἴ μοι παρείκοι....

....

νικᾶν γε μέντοι πανταχοῦ χρῄζων ἔφυν,
πλὴν ἐς σέ· νῦν δὲ σοί γ' ἑκὼν ἐκστήσομαι.

Victory is what counts, he says in essence, and what you think means less than nothing. Rather than trouble to persuade Philoctetes, he threatens him with an alternative that is no alternative. ἢν μὴ ἕρπῃς ἑκών (985), he says, I will take you under compulsion. Philoctetes' wants could not be of less account in Odysseus' eyes. Finally Odysseus abruptly turns and leaves, taking the bow with him, considering or pretending to consider the object more important than the man. Even if nothing more were said, Neoptolemus, and the audience, must realize that Philoctetes could not possibly have any desire for renown among men of whom such a man as Odysseus is a leader, or wish to serve alongside them. But the point is explicitly made. Odysseus makes one small effort to appeal to Philoctetes' ambition for glory (995-99):

Philoctetes: ἡμᾶς μὲν ὡς δούλους σαφῶς
πατὴρ ἄρ' ἐξέφυσεν οὐδ' ἐλευθέρους.
Odysseus: οὐκ, ἀλλ' ὁμοίους τοῖς ἀρίστοισιν, μεθ' ὧν
Τροίαν σ' ἑλεῖν δεῖ καὶ κατασκάψαι βίᾳ.
Philoctetes: οὐδέποτέ γ' · οὐδ' ἢν χρῆ με πᾶν παθεῖν κακόν.

Philoctetes does not consider these proposed companions to be "the best." As he has said, the best are all dead—Achilles, Ajax, Antilochus, Patroclus—and the survivors are the Atreidae, Odysseus, Thersites, and their ilk (341-452; see above, pp. 34-35). Philoctetes has no sense of fellow-feeling whatever with the Greeks who stand before Troy, neither a desire for their esteem nor a feeling of duty toward them. To him they are the enemy, who have spurned him and deserve of him hatred unto death (1200-02):

Philoctetes: ἐρρέτω "Ιλιον, οἵ θ' ὑπ' ἐκείνῳ
πάντες ὅσοι τόδ' ἔτλασαν ἐμοῦ ποδὸς
ἄρθρον ἀπῶσαι.

Philoctetes' revulsion from his former comrades seems all the stronger because of the strong need he manifests for friendship throughout the play. It is ironic in the extreme that the man on whose lips early in the play the word φίλος so often appears is brought utterly to reject the friendship available to him; while the self-centered Odysseus, who betrays no care for anything but success, is said by the bow's theft to have effected κοινὰν ... ἐς φίλους ἀρωγάν (1145). The conflict within Philoctetes between his righteous hatred and his longing for companionship is best seen in the kommos following Odysseus' departure with the bow (1081-1217). Here he alternately rejects the chorus' overtures and begs them not to leave him, until in desperation he turns to death as the only solution to the impasse (1204-17).

Almost all critics, even those who believe that his anger over his wrongs is fully justified, blame Philoctetes for this intransigence, which seems to be a sterile rejection of the present good out of anger over wrongs of the past. Even if he scorns honor from the Greeks at Troy, the choice of continued suffering when cure is possible, the rejection of a life of action and accomplishment in favor of death, appears to be nothing but futile perversity.[87] Neoptolemus' words during this last effort to win Philoctetes over lend a certain credence to this interpretation (1318-21; quoted above, p. 13):

> ὅσοι δ' ἑκουσίοισιν ἔγκεινται βλάβαις,
> ὥσπερ σύ, τούτοις οὔτε συγγνώμην ἔχειν
> δίκαιόν ἐστιν οὔτ' ἐποικτίρειν τινά.
> σὺ δ' ἠγρίωσαι.

Neoptolemus seems to be saying, You close your eyes to the good while you cling to the bad of the past, but he is not. He no longer believes, as he did, that the gods are compensating Philoctetes and he does not say so. He argues only that one must make the best of things: It is necessary for men to endure the τύχαι given to them by the gods (1316-17). And I know that these things are fated to come about (1336-42). To be sure he does mention the two advantages to be gained by acceptance—the cure and the winning of fame. But, as his subsequent consent to abet Philoctetes in his savagery shows, Neoptolemus does not believe that these are unalloyed goods which any sane man would choose (see above pp. 31 and 39). At this point he is playing the part of a realist, not an idealist; and when he later says to Philoctetes, ὦ τᾶν, διδάσκου

---

[87] For instance Knox, 140, says, "Philoctetes' stubbornness condemns him to inaction, to ineffective suffering; he clings to the mood of vengeful self-pity, which has been his comfort for ten lonely years, and plays the role of victim rather than hero." Harsh [above, note 34], 408: "Philoctetes' determination to sacrifice health and glory to vengeance is irrational and perverse."

Linforth [above, note 16], 148, and Fuqua [above, note 48], 187-89, are the only critics I know who have fully appreciated that Philoctetes' yielding would be a compromise of his integrity.

μὴ θρασύνεσθαι κακοῖς (1387), he is speaking the language of survival, not of honor.

The critics who blame Philoctetes for his persistent rejection of the gods' restoration of him to society would be right, and Neoptolemus' change of heart would be inexplicable, if all of the evil were in the past. The question whether the gods' compensation to Philoctetes is adequate or commensurate with his past suffering would be meaningless. Granted that it is true that Philoctetes has no interest in helping the Greeks at Troy or in winning renown among them; at any rate, to be returned to society and to be cured surely would be preferable to his grim struggle for existence on the desert island. It is surprising that Neoptolemus does not say to Philoctetes, Things have changed; your troubles are over, or something to this effect. Instead he says, We have to make the best of what the gods impose upon us. Perhaps he already is beginning to see, even before Philoctetes' reply, that things really have not changed all that much.

The "plot of persecution," as I have called it, is common enough in the modern cinema, as well as in other forms of melodrama, where there often is a reversal at the end, the hero saved, the villains punished, and the audience' faith in the goodness of things restored. It may seem that in this play things are thus set right in the end. However, Philoctetes himself does not think so. He resists "salvation" almost to the last extremity. Perhaps this stubborn defiance is mere irrational hatred, conditioned by his long suffering. But his answer of refusal to Neoptolemus is quite cogent and to the point. Is this benefit you are talking about a benefit to me or to the Atreidae? he asks (1384). This is a crucial point, and one which to my knowledge has been entirely ignored by critics. Villainy is not punished in this play but rewarded. Philoctetes is being taken to Troy so that he may bring succour and and eventually triumph to those who nine years before so cold-bloodedly abandoned him to torment. Earlier in the play (446-52) Philoctetes complained bitterly that the gods seem to take special care of villains, and he concluded with the question (451-52; see above, p. 35), How can I praise the gods ... when I find them evil? Nevertheless, despite the bitter resentment to which his experience forces him, Philoctetes is no Capaneus, and he cannot bring himself to believe, even when assured by Neoptolemus, that the gods could really will anything so unfair. Aren't you ashamed before the gods to

say such things? he asks Neoptolemus (1382). However, Neoptolemus, and we the audience, since we know the myth, know
that this is precisely what the gods have decreed; and it is difficult
to see how we can escape the conclusion that the gods' concern for
justice is at best nonchalant.

Still, Philoctetes will be saved. It may be true that the gods'
dispensation of justice is capricious, and that they are continuing
to "take excellent care of the wicked" (see line 447). Nevertheless,
it may seem that so far as Philoctetes is directly and personally
affected the play does provide a reversal of misfortune. The gods
will cure his foot and return him to the society of men that he so
poignantly desires. To be sure this is a bare half-step toward a just
order of things. But, as Neoptolemus has told him, you have to
accept the evils of life and take the good wherever you can find it.
If the return to the Greek army will profit Philoctetes, what is his
refusal but a self-righteous and self-defeating insistence upon having
all or nothing?

It should be perfectly clear that Philoctetes is willing to accept a
great deal less than all. He asks only to be returned to his homeland
and his father. He wants nothing more than to forget about Troy
and the Greek army forever. He is willing to live with his wound
and to forego all thought of vengeance upon Odysseus and the
Atreidae, much as he desires it. If he never shows any interest in or
entertains any hope of the possibility of a cure, it is because it will
bring more bad than good.[88] When he goes to Troy his physical
suffering will be relieved, but the worse wound to his self-respect
will be too much to bear. At Troy he will not just be returned to
the fellowship of men, but to a special company—that of his
tormentors. He is being impressed against his will into a fellowship that is totally repugnant to him. Neoptolemus sums up
Philoctetes' attitude toward these men in a statement early in
the play; it is a statement that is disingenuous but one which
Philoctetes takes at face value and with which he implicitly agrees
(454-58):

τὸ λοιπὸν ἤδη τηλόθεν τό τ' Ἴλιον
καὶ τοὺς Ἀτρείδας εἰσορῶν φυλάξομαι·

---

[88] Indeed, earlier in the play, before he has been told of his destined cure,
he mentions it as a hypothetical possibility and says that vengeance is more
important to him: εἰ δ' ἴδοιμ' ὀλωλότας / τούτους, δοκοῖμ' ἂν τῆς νόσου
πεφευγέναι (1043-44).

ὅπου θ' ὁ χείρων τἀγαθοῦ μεῖζον σθένει
κἀποφθίνει τὰ χρηστὰ χὠ δειλὸς κρατεῖ,
τούτους ἐγὼ τοὺς ἄνδρας οὐ στέρξω ποτέ.

How does a man vindicate his self-respect, in what terms does he explain himself to himself when he consents to become part of an order of things in which a man like Odysseus becomes a success, a pious man, a favorite of the gods? How does he acquire success himself and respect from others? By outdoing them in ruthlessness and cynicism? No, says Philoctetes to Neoptolemus, Let us repudiate these evil men, κοὐ κακοὺς ἐπωφελῶν / δόξεις ὅμοιος τοῖς κακοῖς πεφυκέναι (1371-72). In particular, what character does a man have who, for the sake of expediency, will ignore the harm done to him by his worst enemy and fight by the enemy's side? Philoctetes says to Neoptolemus (1362-67):

> I wonder at this in you. For you should never yourself have gone to Troy .... These men outraged you, stealing your father's prize of honor from you. Will you then fight as their ally and force me to do this?

Something more humiliating is demanded of Philoctetes than that he abandon merely abstract and impersonal notions of right and wrong. He is asked in effect to embrace his enemies. He must return to Troy on their terms, to accomplish an end that they desire, not he. He must deny the validity of his own feelings of outrage and renounce all claim to justice. This is very near to the ultimate degradation. Eyes of mine, he says (1354-57), having seen all these things (his wrongs) how can you endure to see me consorting with these sons of Atreus, who have destroyed me, or the damned son of Laertes?

And so Neoptolemus consents to take Philoctetes home, in conscious defiance of the gods' will. Because even after having suffered so much, and having been brought so low, even in the face of death Philoctetes holds on to his last ounce of dignity. And because the justice of the gods is a tawdry thing, indiscriminately punishing the good and rewarding the evil. Only in Philoctetes does Neoptolemus believe himself to have found unwavering devotion to principle. It is to this that he responds, and in consenting to return Philoctetes to his homeland he determines to break the pattern of the past: for the first time in almost ten years some-

thing will be done that Philoctetes wants. Philoctetes' past depriva-
tion has so humbled him that he is convinced that his personal
wishes are of little value; they have been of little concern to others
(see above, pp. 16-18). But his return to the Greek army—heaven's
purpose—will require of him even further effacement: the relin-
quishment of his most deeply-held feelings and convictions. However, he is not brought so low that he cannot steadfastly resist this
final surrender of his human dignity. And Neoptolemus' response
is an acknowledgement of his successful defense of his status as a
volitional creature.

* * *

I should say, almost successful. For now I refer, of course, to the
deus ex machina. Those who have argued that *Philoctetes* is not a
tragedy have been right, but this is not because it has a happy
ending.[89] Only the reprobates have reason to rejoice, and when for
the first time Philoctetes is about to get what he wants, or what
he is willing to settle for from life, suddenly it is snatched from
him. The ingredients of tragedy are there. Neoptolemus' decision,
if carried to accomplishment, would be the classic tragic decision:
he makes a moral choice to commit an act in full knowledge that
it is directly contrary to the decree of the gods (not to mention
the fact that it is tantamount to a renunciation of his own chance
for fame and glory). Without the *deus ex machina* to save them from
themselves Neoptolemus and Philoctetes are about to embark on
a collision course with the forces governing the universe. It is an
act that is ennobling because of its very desperation. What denatures
the tragedy at its crisis is that Philoctetes' defiance of the gods is

---

[89] Kott [above, note 41], 181, says that the ending is unhappy but he does
not remark upon the bitter irony of Philoctetes' reversal. Nor does he think
that the words of the *deus ex machina* are, as I have argued, irrelevant to the
preceding action. Philoctetes is an archetype of man's suffering, marked for
this role by actively malignant gods (168, 181) and by historical necessity
(170, 172, 183). It is of suffering that Heracles speaks (181). The *ex machina*
ending seems not to be a surprise to the audience or a shock to its expectations, but to provide a kind of inevitable climax of the play's bleak pessimism.
For the gods are destroyers (168, 172) who, in Kott's scheme of things, use
those chosen by them as the agents of their destruction as well as their
victims. Thus the suffering in question is not only that experienced by
Philoctetes in the past but the suffering of Troy, which symbolizes the
violence continually suffered by mankind (181-83). So Kott says, but he
points to no evidence of such pacifist concern for Troy's well-being. See my
remarks in note 41 on the bias of Kott's interpretation.

not so conscious or so determined as Neoptolemus thinks it. Philoctetes, in spite of all assurances, does not really believe that it can be true that the gods want anything so unjust as his return to Odysseus and the Atreidae.[90] Philoctetes may think that no force on earth can make him go to Troy against his wishes—and he seems willing to face the alternative of death by starvation— but when confronted with inescapable direct evidence of the gods' will he has not the moral strength to resist. And why should he? He is only a man. Nevertheless, in what light does this cast his brave words (1197-99), Never, never [will I come], not if Zeus should threaten me with his thunderbolt? Sophocles is not making of Philoctetes an empty poseur, a burlesque figure. When he says these words Philoctetes means them with the highest seriousness, and in their context they are both dramatic and awesome. Even so, they lend to his later quick acceptance of Zeus' orders a grim irony, and it is an irony that recognizes the true ratio of man's strength to the gods'.

The *deus ex machina*, far from being anticlimactic or "external" to the drama, is its logical conclusion. The play emphasizes Philoctetes' suffering, his humiliation, and his helpless ineffectuality. The *deus* not only imposes on him a necessity so degrading that he considers it worse than death; it demands and receives an implicit obedience that mocks his earlier unyielding defiance. And in an even more significant way the *deus* confirms Philoctetes in his futility and provides an appropriate conclusion. Early in the play Philoctetes suffers intensely and despairs of the possibility of physical salvation, but he is able to take comfort at least in his

---

[90] When Odysseus says to him, This is the will of Zeus and I am only his servant (989-990), Philoctetes answers, You hateful creature, what lies you invent. Pleading the authority of the gods you make the gods out liars (991-92). Philoctetes does indeed believe that perhaps the gods have imposed upon the Greeks a need for him; but he believes, as the following words to Odysseus show, that it is a need that the gods will allow to go unsatisfied (1035-42):

You will perish for having wronged me if the gods have a concern for justice. And I know that they do, since never would you have sailed on this mission for one so wretched unless a divine goad were driving you. But oh fatherland and gods who watch over us punish them all . . . .

Later he says to Neoptolemus who tells him of the god's will (1382; see above, p. 45), Aren't you ashamed before the gods to say such things? Neoptolemus is not ashamed because he is telling the simple truth, as everyone but Philoctetes knows.

righteous hatred. If Odysseus continues to be successful, at least his actions have branded him a worthless rogue worthy of the scorn of honorable men like Philoctetes himself. The play is full of expressions of metaphysical uncertainty. Why should the gods have allowed Philoctetes to suffer so? Why should the gods have allowed the good to perish on the battlefield and the evil to survive and prosper? These doubts about the existence of the gods' justice seem confirmed when Philoctetes' bow is taken from him and he is abandoned, as he thinks, to die. Surely knavery again is on the point of triumph. Nevertheless, Philoctetes' moral firmness never wavers; and the sense of angry disillusion which the audience feels at this point must surely be tempered by admiration, as well as by the reassurance that the existence of moral order in the world is not entirely to be despaired of. If there is no cosmic justice at least there is hope in man, who can defend his own values. For a short while Philoctetes raises himself above the status of victim. When the gods require him to renounce his hatred and to reward those whom he knows to be evil, what they require is a renunciation of his last comfort, his claim to righteousness. If, when the gods ordered him to go to Troy, they thought worthy to indicate to him a Transcendent Reason—a reason which he had not taken into consideration, which superseded his objections—he still would be forced to embrace his despised enemies, but his consciousness of doing the right thing would survive intact to compensate him for his humiliation. But the gods do not even condescend to reason with him. The *deus* offers him nothing more than the two rewards, (1) You will be healed, and (2) You will win glory among the Greeks, which he has rejected before.

Philoctetes' reasons for refusing to go to Troy and his desperate defense of his moral position must—for I believe that this is a successful play—engage the audience' most intense interest and sympathy. But his objections fail to engage the gods' interest at all. The gods ignore the action on the human plane as casually as if it had never happened. The last five lines (1440-44) of Heracles' speech are an adjuration to piety, but it is difficult to see how the *deus ex machina* can have inspired any piety even in a contemporary audience. The gods' complete lack of concern for what Philoctetes thinks, for his moral outrage and his anguish, shows clearly that they have no concern for him except as an instrument of the destiny that they have decreed. And to the extent that the men observing this play participate vicariously in Philoctetes' experiences, the gods' summary disregard of Philoctetes' needs becomes a disregard of their own. The sudden reversal of events demanded by the *deus* and Philoctetes' ready acceptance disappoint their emotional expectations. Philoctetes' failure becomes a paradigm of the frustration and futility of mankind.

Printed in the United States
By Bookmasters